forging
AHEAD

PITTSBURGH AT 250

1908: The city celebrated its 150th anniversary with a flotilla and parades, and by replacing gas-light lamps with electric models. Cornerstones were laid for what is now Soldiers & Sailors Military Museum and Memorial and for State Hall, the first building to be erected on what then was the new Oakland campus for the University of Pittsburgh.

Trib Total Media
Pittsburgh Tribune-Review
503 Martindale Street
Pittsburgh, Pennsylvania 15212

Richard M. Scaife Publisher, Inc.

Printed by Reed & Witting Co.

ISBN: 978-0-615-24532-4

Printed in Pittsburgh, Pennsylvania

Forging Ahead: Pittsburgh at 250

Richard A. Monti AND **Sandra Skowron**
Editors

James M. Kubus
Creative Director

Elizabeth K. Jackson
Designer

Steven Adams
Photo Editor

Dean M. Beattie
Digital Imaging Specialist

Carol Shrefler
Project Manager

Marilyn Anobile AND **Charles Rondinelli**
Copy Editors

Robin Acton, Rob Biertempfel, Jeremy Boren, Brian Bowling, David Brown, Scott Brown, Alice Carter, Andrew Conte, Ron DaParma, Sandra Fischione Donovan, Debra Erdley, Luis Fabregas, Allison Heinrichs, Mark Houser, Mark Kanny, Dirk Kaufman, F.A. Krift, Daveen Rae Kurutz, Tony LaRussa, Kim Leonard, Jack Markowitz, Samantha Morgan, Joe Napsha, Tom Olson, Jenny Paul, Bonnie Pfister, Carl Prine, Mike Prisuta, Jennifer Reeger, Jim Ritchie, Richard Robbins, Joe Rutter, Kurt Shaw, Craig Smith, Joe Starkey, Dan Stefano, Rick Stouffer, Chris Togneri, Laura Van Wert, Justin Vellucci, Mike Wereschagin, Rick Wills, Salena Zito, Bill Zlatos
Writers

CONTENTS

PREFACE

In the 1750s, Western Pennsylvania became the focus of the Western world.

The first shots of the French and Indian War were fired here and led to the first global conflict, one which upset the balance of power in Europe and the New World.

That volley also helped to unleash colonial passions that provoked America's War for Independence, a revolution in self-government that would sweep the world.

The frontier outpost of Fort Pitt and the eventual settlement of Pittsburgh soon became a focus of the new American nation, a starting point for tens of thousands of settlers surging west.

In decades to come, the city grew into one of the nation's centers of industry and invention, one of its primary immigrant "melting pots." Many of its people grew, too, into national or international figures who changed government, industry, science and technology, medical care, education, the arts – and much more – for America and for the world.

Two hundred and fifty years later, Pittsburgh remains central to American life.

It has traded smoky industries for high-tech firms and university research programs that attract global talent, yet it remains headquarters to numerous national and international companies. Its people continue to change the course of human life, here and abroad.

Forging Ahead: Pittsburgh at 250 captures the essence of one of America's most storied, beautiful and important cities. It looks at many of the people who helped to build our city, and some who left here to change the world. It examines many of the events that shaped our future, along with little-known facts and footnotes that make our city unique. And it includes historic photographs, illustrations and artwork, as well as up-to-date images of the city.

We hope you enjoy our view of Pittsburgh and the people who have kept it forging ahead.

— The news staff of the Pittsburgh Tribune-Review
and Trib Total Media

1755: This 1856 oil painting, "Evening of Braddock's Defeat" by William Coventry Wall, shows Pittsburgh as wilderness.

CHAPTER 1

SENATOR JOHN HEINZ HISTORY CENTER

forging
ahead

"As I got down before the Canoe, I spent some Time in viewing the Rivers, and the Land in the Fork; which I think extremely well situated for a Fort, as it has the absolute Command of both Rivers.* The Land at the Point is 20 or 25 Feet above the common Surface of the Water; and a considerable Bottom of flat, well-timbered Land all around it, very convenient for Building: The Rivers are each a Quarter of a Mile, or more, across, and run here very near at right Angles: Aligany bearing N.E. and Monongahela S.E. The former of these two is a very rapid and swift running Water; the other deep and still, without any perceptible Fall."

– GEORGE WASHINGTON FROM HIS JOURNAL, ABOUT NOVEMBER 23, 1753; PRINTED IN WILLIAMSBURG, VIRGINIA, 1754.

*WASHINGTON NOTED THAT THE ALIGANY AND OHIO WERE THE SAME RIVER

1

The rivers were always important.

The British, French and Native Americans each wanted the area that came to be called Pittsburgh because of its location. The rivers were vital for trade and transportation.

Pittsburgh has been reborn many times during its 250 years, and the three rivers have been key to the transformation – from wilderness to commercial center to an industrial powerhouse and now as a high-tech city capitalizing on its natural beauty.

In 1758, British forces led by General John Forbes captured Fort Duquesne from the French after carving a highway over the Alleghenies to the forks of the Ohio River. He renamed the camp, Pittsburgh.

After the nation's independence, the frontier town became the Gateway to the West. It was the starting point for the epic journey of Meriwether Lewis and William Clark in 1803 to explore the Northwest Territory.

In 1845, a fire destroyed a third of the city. Rebuilding brought innovation. John Roebling, a German immigrant living in Saxonburg, replaced the burned Monongahela River bridge using his then-fledgling wire-rope suspension design. Although his span was replaced by the Smithfield Street bridge in 1881, it became a model for one of America's most iconic images, the Brooklyn Bridge.

Early 1900s: A view of the Point from Mount Washington showing the first Point Bridge spanning the Monongahela River on the right and the Manchester Bridge on the left spanning the Allegheny River.

1906: Horse-drawn carriages and electric street cars are the primary modes of transportation along bustling Liberty Avenue.

The Bessemer process gave birth to the modern steel industry, bringing a flood of immigrants who created a mosaic of culture and traditions. The Bessemer process, developed during the 1850s, was the first method for making steel cheaply and in large quantities. Air is blown through molten metal in a furnace that looks like a cement mixer. The impurities are burned out, and the purified molten metal can be poured into molds.

Some of the nation's bloodiest labor conflicts were here. The nation was stunned when 45 people died in 1877 during a strike against the Pennsylvania Railroad. In 1892, three Pinkerton detectives and seven workers were killed in a battle at the Carnegie Steel Company Works in Homestead.

From 1880 to 1960, Pittsburgh was the hearth of a nation. At the height of World War II, the Pittsburgh area produced 27 percent of the nation's steel.

But the city bore the scars of the Industrial Age.

After World War II ended, city leaders reinstituted smoke-control ordinances suspended during the conflict. River discharges were regulated. Businessman Richard King Mellon and Mayor David L. Lawrence paved the way for the city's renaissance.

By the 1980s, Pittsburgh's backbone of steel turned to rust.

Today's renaissance is being built on medicine, computer technology, artificial intelligence, robotics and life sciences. Universities are conducting world-class research. New companies are innovators in information technology. The beauty of the rivers is celebrated.

Pittsburgh remains a gateway, just as it always has been.

.the first
industries

SHIPBUILDING

Henry Clay, the 19th-century American lawmaker and statesman, got a chuckle from members of the House of Representatives when he told a story about a ship built in "Pittsburg" that sailed across the Atlantic to a European port.

When the ship's captain gave his papers to a foreign customs official, the official insisted no such American port as "Pittsburg" existed and threatened to seize the vessel for phony papers. The captain produced a map to show the inland port where the confluence of the Allegheny and Monongahela rivers formed the Ohio, showing how the ship was routed to the Mississippi River and Gulf of Mexico.

"The custom officer...would have as soon believed that the vessel had performed a voyage from the moon," Clay noted.

Claimed by the British in 1758, Pittsburgh was a shipbuilding center by 1761.

The most famous "big boat" built here was the 55-foot-long keelboat for the Lewis and Clark Expedition launched in August 1803. The *New Orleans*, the first steamboat to ply the western waters, was launched from Pittsburgh in 1811.

During World War II, the shipbuilding industry flourished with wartime vessels produced on the banks of the Ohio River at Dravo Corporation, on Neville Island, and at the American Bridge Company Division of United States Steel Corporation in Ambridge, Beaver County.

LIBRARY AND ARCHIVES DIVISION, SENATOR JOHN HEINZ HISTORY CENTER

c. 1950: Dravo Corporation's Engineering Works Division at Neville Island operates one of the largest inland waterway shipyards in the United States. This location also includes a side-haul marine repair facility. Some of the products manufactured at this facility include hopper, tank and deck barges (pictured here under construction), towboats, tugs, dredges, and special-purpose vessels. Dravo has launched more than 6,000 hulls since it entered the shipbuilding business in 1915.

EARLY METALS

Pittsburgh's earliest metal makers were highly skilled, often British, craftsmen eager to prosper in a growing region rich in natural resources and waterways.

Scotsman John Fraser is regarded as the first. He was a gunsmith for George Washington's Virginia regiment, working at a forge he built in 1749 at the mouth of Turtle Creek near Braddock.

George Anshutz built the city's first blast furnace in 1792 in what now is Shadyside, though it ran only two years because of problems securing iron ore.

Industry developed here because of Pittsburgh's location on the Ohio River. Travelers resupplied here before continuing west. Small factories grew in the city and outlying areas through the early 1800s.

The Jeffery Scaife Tin and Japanned Ware Manufactory started business in 1802 in the Diamond area of Downtown; the Juniata Iron Works and Rolling Mill was founded in 1824 in what is now the Strip District; and Sligo Rolling Mill in 1825 in what is now the South Side.

High-quality bituminous coal also gave Pittsburgh an edge because of the high temperatures needed to melt iron and other metals.

Coke production that started in the 1840s in Connellsville provided an even better energy source.

Steel was a minor industry before the Civil War. The 1870s brought transition from small factories to huge integrated mills, housing several processes for mass production.

WILLIAM J. GAUGHAN COLLECTION, ARCHIVES SERVICES CENTER, UNIVERSITY OF PITTSBURGH

c. 1892-95: Workers at Carnegie Steel Company's Homestead Works tend the 32-inch slabbing mill, which produced metal plate for the "The Great White Fleet" of the United States Navy. These ships fought in the Spanish-American War in 1898 and later sailed around the world in a display of sea power. The defense contract enabled Andrew Carnegie to expand the Homestead Works. The slabbing mill was still in operation when the works closed in 1986. It was demolished in 1990.

COAL

Early coal mining in Pittsburgh was a casual affair.

Charles Lyell, a noted English geologist, visited the area in the 1840s and was "truly astonished" at the "richness of the seams of coal which appeared everywhere on the flanks of the hills and at the bottoms of the valleys, and which are accessible in a degree I have never witnessed elsewhere."

That easy access to what became known as the Pittsburgh seam allowed individuals and families to "mine" coal by knocking off the outcroppings and then digging shallow pits. There are several accounts of people carelessly starting underground fires by getting a flame too close to the exposed seam. When that happened, they simply moved on to the next outcropping because the fires could last for years.

In a geological survey published in 1884, J. Sutton Wall describes hundreds of small mines that operated or had operated in the area. By the middle of the 19th century, factories and foundries would become the main customers of Pittsburgh coal, but for those early mines, the main customers were people who needed heating fuel.

Wall quotes an F. Cumming who wrote about Pittsburgh in 1804. Cumming said the coal mining operations would send around wagons that would go door-to-door selling coal at 5 cents a bushel.

COAL MINERS, PITTSBURGH, PA.   8066.

Early room-and-pillar mining relied on manual labor to cut the coal at the front of the mine. The coal was then hauled from the mine by wagons drawn by horse or donkey.

1914: Employees of the Cunningham Glass Factory located at 900 Carson Street. William Cunningham founded the company in 1850 and made window glass, flint glass and druggist glassware. Most of the glass tableware in the United States was produced on the South Side.

GLASS

Pittsburgh may be known as the "Steel City," but almost eight decades before Andrew Carnegie opened his first steel plant, the region's first two glass manufacturing plants were operating.

Glass is the great untold story about Pittsburgh.

In 1797, the Pittsburgh Glassworks was established at the foot of the Monongahela River near the present site of the Duquesne Incline on the South Side. That same year, businessman Albert Gallatin's glass factory began operating along the Monongahela in New Geneva, Fayette County.

Gallatin saw that Pittsburgh served as a strategic "jumping off point" for settlers headed West. There were other factors spurring the region's growth as a glassmaking center. There was plenty of coal for fuel and the presence of the iron industry.

By 1840, Pittsburgh was considered the pressed-glass capital of the world.

By the early 1900s, more than 100 glass factories were in Western Pennsylvania and, by 1920, an estimated 80 percent of American glass was made in Western Pennsylvania, West Virginia and Ohio.

Pittsburgh glass has graced the tables of five United States presidents and the crown of the Statue of Liberty.

WESTERN PENNSYLVANIA counties

Allegheny

Created on September 24, 1788, from parts of Westmoreland and Washington counties and named for the Allegheny River. The county seat, Pittsburgh, was named by General John Forbes in 1758 in honor of William Pitt, a British statesman.

2008 Population: About 1.2 million

Pittsburgh's distinctive Allegheny County Courthouse

JOE APPEL/TRIBUNE-REVIEW

Armstrong

Created on March 12, 1800, and named for American Revolutionary War General John Armstrong. Kittanning, the county seat, got its name from a Delaware Indian village at the same location.

2008 Population: About 70,000

Armstrong County Courthouse

B.F. HENRY/TRIBUNE-REVIEW

Butler County Courthouse seen from Diamond Square

AIMEE OBIDZINSKI/TRIBUNE-REVIEW

Butler

Created on March 12, 1800, from part of Allegheny County and named for Revolutionary War hero General Richard Butler. The county seat is Butler.

2008 Population: About 183,000

Beaver

Created on March 12, 1800, from Washington and Allegheny counties and named for the Beaver River. The county seat is Beaver, which may have been named for King Beaver, chief of a Delaware tribe.

2008 Population: About 175,000

Fishing at Brady's Run Lake

CHRISTOPHER HORNER/TRIBUNE-REVIEW

Fayette

Created on September 26, 1783, and named for the Marquis de Lafayette. The county seat was first called Beeson's-town, then called Uniontown in reference to the federal Union.

2008 Population: About 146,000

Frank Lloyd Wright's Fallingwater

SEAN STIPP/TRIBUNE-REVIEW

Somerset

Created on April 17, 1795, and named for Somersetshire, England. The county seat is Somerset.

2008 Population: About 78,000

An Amish farm

S.C. SPANGLER/TRIBUNE-REVIEW

Greene

Created on February 9, 1796, and named for American Revolutionary War General Nathanael Greene. The county seat, Waynesburg, was named for Major General Anthony Wayne, Revolutionary War general and Indian fighter.

2008 Population: About 40,000

A Greene County farm

GUY WATHEN/TRIBUNE-REVIEW

Washington

Created on March 28, 1781, and named for George Washington. The county seat is Washington.

2008 Population: About 206,000

Meadowcroft's one-room schoolhouse

TRIBUNE-REVIEW

Lawrence

Created on March 20, 1849, and named for Oliver Hazard Perry's flagship, which engaged the British in 1813 in the Battle of Lake Erie. The county seat, New Castle, may have been named for Newcastle, England, or New Castle, Delaware.

2008 Population: About 92,000

McConnell's Mill State Park

KEITH HODAN/TRIBUNE-REVIEW

Westmoreland

Created on February 26, 1773, and named for a county in England. Greensburg, the county seat, was named for American Revolutionary War General Nathanael Greene.

2008 Population: About 366,000

Westmoreland Courthouse rotunda

BARRY REEGER/TRIBUNE-REVIEW

evolution
OF THE
region

The geography that made Pittsburgh a vital location had to be harnessed and conquered if the city was to prosper.

In early Pittsburgh, rivers were the only superhighway – for a while.

In 1803, the first shipments of coal went to Philadelphia via the Ohio and Mississippi rivers, the Gulf of Mexico and the Atlantic Ocean, but the wilderness road cut by General John Forbes in 1758 was becoming a vital artery. By 1804, stagecoaches were crossing the state in the "speedy" time of six days.

Fifty years later, a passenger could make the trip by rail in 13 hours.

When the first river bridge opened in 1818 over the Monongahela River at Smithfield Street, it was such a momentous occasion that cannons boomed, flags waved and the workers celebrated with a banquet and many toasts. Walking across it cost 2 cents.

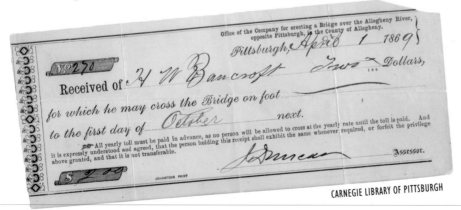

CARNEGIE LIBRARY OF PITTSBURGH

1896: Toll bridge receipt

2002: The Roberto Clemente, the Rachel Carson and the Andy Warhol bridges, which link Downtown and the North Side, are called the Three Sisters Bridges. The Clemente Bridge, in the foreground, was honored as the "Most Beautiful Steel Bridge of 1928" by the American Institute of Steel Construction. The sloping roof of the nearby David L. Lawrence Convention Center mimics the slope of these bridges.

CANALS

In the early 1820s, the National Road from Baltimore to Wheeling and the Erie Canal across New York state threatened Pittsburgh's position as the Gateway to the West.

The solution: a canal connecting Pittsburgh with Philadelphia.

Authorized by the General Assembly in 1824, the Pennsylvania Canal opened along its entire length 10 years later. The feat included the construction of the world-famous Allegheny Portage Railroad – a series of 10 inclines to carry canal boats on rail cars over Allegheny Mountain from Hollidaysburg and Johnstown.

The Pennsylvania Canal reinvigorated Pittsburgh's iron industry and doubled the volume of trade moving back and forth across Pennsylvania. Also important to the iron industry was the Erie Extension Canal, which was the major means of travel between Pittsburgh and Erie starting in the 1840s.

The Chesapeake and Ohio Canal, a man-made river built in the early 1800s, connected coal fields in the Allegheny Mountains to East Coast markets for more than eight decades. Today, the 184.5-mile waterway is a popular recreation attraction within the 20,000-acre Chesapeake and Ohio National Historic Park.

National Park Service historians estimate that it took 22 years for 35,000 stonemasons and laborers to build the canal and its 74 locks and dams. When it opened in 1836, the canal enabled heavy boats – pulled by mule teams on the tow path – to maneuver through successively lower levels of terrain from Cumberland, Maryland, to Washington, D.C., along a route parallel to the unnavigable Potomac River.

The canal era came to a close starting in the 1850s with the coming of the railroads.

1913: Horses and trolleys compete for space as they make their way down Forbes Avenue.

ROADS

In 1758, British General John Forbes and his army used brute strength and axes to carve a trail out of nearly 300 miles of Pennsylvania wilderness from Philadelphia to Fort Duquesne at the head of the Ohio River during the French and Indian War.

The trail allowed British soldiers to mount a successful attack against the French and gain control of the strategic river confluence. They built Fort Pitt at what would become Point State Park.

The road also made westward settlement easier from Philadelphia and helped ensure that Pittsburgh would be part of Pennsylvania. Virginia also claimed the territory, but Pennsylvania's authority prevailed in 1775.

Today, much of the trail is incorporated into Route 30, the Pennsylvania Turnpike and Forbes Avenue. Other parts have become footpaths that traverse state and county parks.

RAILS

In 1846, the state chartered the Pennsylvania Railroad Company to connect Harrisburg to Pittsburgh and complete cross-state rail service. Only Philadelphia-Lancaster-Harrisburg rail service existed at that time.

Allegheny County and other localities offered money to fund the Pennsylvania Railroad, or PRR, as did private investors. By December 1852, workers built 250 miles of track from Harrisburg to Pittsburgh at a cost of $19 million.

Railroads helped to create Pittsburgh's early suburbs, including Sewickley, East Liberty, Wilkinsburg and Turtle Creek. In 1852, a 54-minute ride to Turtle Creek cost 40 cents roundtrip.

For two years the PRR used the Pennsylvania Canal's Allegheny Portage Railroad, an inconvenient series of inclined planes built against the slopes of the 2,400-foot Allegheny Mountain. In 1854, the PRR completed its own rail line from Altoona around Horseshoe Curve, through a mountaintop tunnel at Gallitzin and down to Johnstown. The canal system was rendered obsolete.

Including acquisition of older, eastern rail lines, the PRR spent $27 million to complete the cross-state railway. Allegheny County defaulted on its bonds in 1858 and surrendered its shares in the company to other investors.

CARNEGIE MUSEUM OF ART, PITTSBURGH; SECOND CENTURY ACQUISITION FUND

1946: A locomotive arrives at the Pennsylvania Railroad's Union Station, Downtown. The United States Post Office and Courthouse, and the Gulf Building are barely visible through the haze in the background.

BRIDGES

Pittsburgh often is called the City of Bridges. With three rivers converging at the Point and a myriad of creeks and streams flowing among the region's hilly terrain, bridges are virtually everywhere.

A federal bridge inventory shows nearly 320 bridges in Pittsburgh. As many as 2,000 in Allegheny County have at least an 8-foot span.

The first bridge crossing a river went up over the Monongahela River in 1818 at the site of the present-day Smithfield Street Bridge. The covered bridge cost $102,000. It was destroyed by the Great Fire in 1845 and replaced with a wire-rope suspension bridge. Today's bridge went up from 1881 to 1883. It was designated a National Historic Landmark in 1976.

The first bridge over the Allegheny opened in 1819 at Federal and Saint Clair streets near the site of the present-day Roberto Clemente Bridge. It was regarded as a great convenience to city dwellers, allowing them easy access to the open spaces of what was then the town of Allegheny.

The Clemente Bridge is one of the Three Sisters bridges crossing the Allegheny River between Downtown and the North Side. The other two are the Rachel Carson Bridge, formerly the Ninth Street Bridge, and the Andy Warhol Bridge, formerly the Seventh Street Bridge.

1912: The Smithfield Street Bridge designed by Austrian engineer Gustav Lindenthal and constructed in 1881 initially had only one lane, but in 1889 a second deck was added, doubling its size. The deck contained a double track of rails for horse-drawn streetcars. In 1899 the deck was widened to accommodate electric streetcars; the rails were removed between 1994 and 1996 when the bridge was completely renovated and the former rail space was opened for cars.

This was the second of four bridges that were built at present-day Sixth Street, Downtown, across the Allegheny River. The multi-span suspension bridge was built in 1859 by John A. Roebling. The two main spans were 344 feet each. The main cables were 7.5 inches in diameter and composed of seven strands of 700 wires each, and weighed 115 pounds per foot.

1902: View of the Union Bridge from the Point. It was a wooden toll bridge built in 1875. It was demolished in 1907 because of its low clearance over the Allegheny River.

1889: The first Point Bridge was built from 1876 to 1877 over the Monongahela River. The stiffened chain suspension bridge was designed by Edward Hemberl of the American Bridge Company. It connected Water Street, now Fort Pitt Boulevard, to an area near the lower station of the Duquesne Incline on East Carson Street. A bridge was constructed beside it from 1925 to 1927. Upon its completion, the Point Bridge was dismantled.

1903: Gustav Lindenthal's Seventh Street Bridge built in 1885 was a complex suspension bridge using trusses to stabilize the double cables that held up the deck. The bridge was replaced in 1926 by a new self-anchored suspension bridge. It is now called the Andy Warhol Bridge.

1951: Traffic crosses from Downtown over the Liberty Bridge, which opened on March 27, 1928, with a mile-long procession of vehicles.

TUNNELS

Like Rome with its catacombs, Pittsburgh can chart its history by the shafts that snake under the earth – in this case, tunnels.

From the opening of the Pennsylvania Canal tunnel just north of Grant Street in 1826 to the construction of the now-buried Pittsburgh and Steubenville rail tunnel a few decades later, on to the automobile tunnels that ushered cars into the city in the first half of the 20th century and back to light rail today, tunnels have been one of the fastest ways for people and products to move in and out of Pittsburgh.

The Liberty Tunnels opened in 1924. They are among the nation's oldest automotive tunnels, completed three years earlier than the Holland Tunnel in New York.

The construction of the Penn-Lincoln Parkway in the 1950s required two sets of tunnels. The Fort Pitt Tunnel on the city's South Side and the Squirrel Hill Tunnel to the east, usher 200,000 cars in and out of the city every day.

The $435 million, roughly mile-long North Shore Connector, which will carry light rail transit under the Allegheny River from the North Shore to Gateway Center when it opens in 2011, will mark the latest chapter in Pittsburgh's underground history.

STEVEN ADAMS/TRIBUNE-REVIEW

MOUNT WASHINGTON TRANSIT TUNNEL

Opened: 1904; rebuilt for use of light rail transit and buses in 1985
Location: On southern bank of Monongahela River. Carries traffic from Carson Street to South Hills.
Length: 3,500 feet

CARNEGIE LIBRARY OF PITTSBURGH

ARMSTRONG TUNNEL

Opened: 1927
Location: Carries South 10th Street from Forbes and Second Avenues, on the northern bank of the Monongahela River, just west of Duquesne University to Carson Street on the South Side.
Length: 1,320 feet

CARNEGIE LIBRARY OF PITTSBURGH

SQUIRREL HILL TUNNEL

Opened: 1953
Location: Carries Interstate 376 under Squirrel Hill on Parkway East, just inside the city's eastern border.
Length: 4,225 feet

WABASH TUNNEL

Opened: 1904 as a railroad tunnel; closed to passenger service in 1931, suffered partial roof collapse in 1946; renovated for mass transit project that never materialized in 1971; renovated again and reopened to high-occupancy vehicles in 2004.
Location: South Side of Pittsburgh above West Carson Street near Station Square to South Hills, under Mount Washington.
Length: 3,450 feet

LIBERTY TUNNELS

Opened: 1924
Location: On the southern bank of the Monongahela River, the tunnel under Mount Washington carries traffic from the Liberty Bridge to the South Hills.
Length: 5,890 feet

FORT PITT TUNNEL

Opened: 1960
Location: Carries Interstate 279 under Mount Washington on the southern bank of the Monongahela River, just north of the Ohio River.
Length: 3,614 feet

NORTH SHORE CONNECTOR TUNNEL

Construction: began 2008, projected completion 2011
Location: Light rail tunnel under the Allegheny River will connect Gateway Center to the North Shore.
Length: approximately 1 mile

1951: The Penn Incline, also called the 17th Street Incline, began operating in 1883 and handled 20-ton coal freight cars. It ceased operation in 1953. The incline operated between the Hill District and the Strip District and was possibly the largest incline ever built. Samuel Diescher, who immigrated to the United States from Hungary in 1866, designed the majority of heavy inclined planes in the United States, including the 17th Street Incline.

INCLINES

In the 19th century, 17 inclines brought Pittsburghers from bluff to valley and back, but only two remain, combining for about 800,000 annual rides.

Termed "funiculars" elsewhere, the Duquesne and Monongahela inclines are passenger railways that use cables to traverse the steep slopes of Mount Washington.

It was difficult to reach the hilltops in the early days. People used steep footpaths or steps. Roads were poor, if they existed at all. Inclines carried horses, wagons, people and even light freight, opening up the hills to settlement.

Erected in 1870 at a cost of $50,000, the Monongahela Incline lowers cars 367 feet at six miles per hour from Mount Washington to a brick building near Station Square. Owned by the Port Authority of Allegheny County, it's one of the steepest funicular journeys nationwide.

The Duquesne Incline, which began operating in 1877, starts at West Carson Street and climbs 400 feet to Grandview Avenue. It closed in 1962, was rebuilt and opened in 1963. It has been held since 1964 by the nonprofit Society for the Preservation of the Duquesne Heights Incline.

Known internationally for its historically precise reconstruction, the Duquesne Incline and its observation deck boast one of the finest views of the Golden Triangle.

FLOOD CONTROL

As a city whose landscape is marked by its rivers, Pittsburgh from its earliest days was no stranger to flooding.

Even the British mopped up after a January flood in 1762, and the French before them in 1756.

The Great Saint Patrick's Day Flood of 1936 is considered the worst natural disaster in Western Pennsylvania. It killed more than 60 people and injured 500, but shaped modern flood-control programs.

The disaster spawned the Flood Control Act of 1936, which has prevented an estimated $11 billion in flood damage. The United States Army Corps of Engineers built 16 flood-control dams, reservoirs and lakes in the Ohio River Basin of Western Pennsylvania and parts of New York, Maryland, Ohio and West Virginia.

It also completed more than 40 flood-control projects to collect water runoff along 72 miles of the Allegheny River and 127.2 miles of the downstream Ohio River. The entire 128.7 miles of the Monongahela are managed by Army Corps projects.

Without flood-control locks and dams, the rivers would have crested at 47.9 feet during Hurricane Agnes in 1972. Instead, they crested at 35.8 feet.

The Conemaugh Dam provides flood protection for the lower Conemaugh Valley, the Kiskiminetas Valley, the lower Allegheny Valley and the upper Ohio River Valley. Water is stored until it can be released without increasing flood conditions downstream. Since its completion in 1952, Conemaugh has prevented more than $2 billion in flood damage.

VISIONARIES

Inventive genius, adventurous personalities and the ability to envision potential propelled a group of 19th-century Western Pennsylvania industrialists to success.

Along the way, they changed the world.

They outdistanced their competitors at every turn as they made a lasting imprint as visionaries. Today, their legacies stand as a tribute to innovation, determination and daring.

Andrew Carnegie

Carnegie was born in Dunfermline, Scotland, on November 25, 1835. A weaver's son, he was 13 in 1848 when his family arrived in Pittsburgh, where he earned $1.20 a week in a cotton mill. Five decades later, the industrialist was lauded as the richest man in the world with a fortune amassed through his ability to embrace new information and anticipate change.

After the Civil War increased demand for iron, he realized the industry's potential and left his Pennsylvania Railroad superintendent's job. With several partners, he founded the Keystone Bridge Works in 1865. Less than a decade later, he opened his first steel works, the Carnegie Steel Company.

Carnegie, a champion for education whose motto was "watch costs and the profits take care of themselves," built an empire that he sold to financier J.P. Morgan for $480 million in 1900. He donated more than $350 million to educational, cultural and peace institutions. Carnegie died August 11, 1919.

Edwin Drake

Drake, born in Greenville, New York, on March 18, 1819, came to Titusville in 1857 when he was hired by the Seneca Oil Company to search for and inspect oil springs. Two years later, his intuitiveness and perseverance secured the region's future as the birthplace of the nation's oil industry.

After several failed attempts to locate a sizable oil reserve, Drake's financial backers deserted him. The former train conductor sought help from friends and kept looking for oil in Titusville.

He pioneered a method of using a drilling pipe to prevent borehole collapsing, which allowed him to dig deeper. On August 27, 1859, he struck oil more than 69 feet below ground.

Many oil refineries were located in Pittsburgh. Drake, who dug only three wells and did not patent his drilling invention, never profited from the oil boom. Impoverished, he died in 1880 in Bethlehem. In 1902 his body was reinterred in Titusville.

Henry Clay Frick

Frick was born December 19, 1849, in West Overton, Westmoreland County. As steel manufacturing burgeoned, the 21-year-old Frick saw opportunity in the region's abundant bituminous coal deposits and borrowed money for a venture to turn coal into coke, an important ingredient used in steelmaking. Frick & Company soon became the world's largest coke producer.

Carnegie and Frick — friends and aggressive entrepreneurs who focused on profits — formed an alliance to guarantee their dominance in the industry. Their reputations dulled in the Homestead Strike of 1892 when they locked out workers protesting long hours and low wages, resulting in violence that killed at least 10 people and injured many more.

He built the Frick Building, the Union Trust Building and William Penn Hotel, all Downtown. His partnership with Carnegie led to the founding of United States Steel Corporation, although their relationship soured because of the Homestead strike and other business decisions.

Frick, an avid art collector, died December 2, 1919.

Henry J. Heinz

Heinz, a food processor who established his company in Sharpsburg in 1869, sold horseradish in clear bottles to prove its quality over the competition. He changed the way Americans eat by providing variety to their diet. Born in Pittsburgh on October 11, 1844, the marketing and food-safety pioneer embraced new developments in technology such as steam-pressure cooking, railroad refrigeration cars and vacuum canning. He moved his company to the North Side in 1882, the same year he patented his famous glass ketchup bottles.

The quality of Heinz's food and his brilliant advertising strategies – the slogan of "57 Varieties" and the green pickle pin, one of the most widely recognized promotional pieces in history – secured his company's future in the international marketplace.

When Heinz died from pneumonia on May 14, 1919, his company included 25 food processing plants and 200 smaller facilities, ranging from container factories to bottling plants to seed farms and offices around the world.

Andrew Mellon

Born in Pittsburgh on March 24, 1855, Mellon, developed his financial expertise as a teenager when he joined his father's banking firm, T. Mellon & Sons. Andrew Mellon helped to organize the Union Trust Company and Union Savings Bank in Pittsburgh, where he expanded his fortune in oil, steel, shipbuilding and construction interests.

Mellon, secretary of the treasury under Presidents Warren G. Harding, Calvin Coolidge and Herbert Hoover, backed successful enterprises in the production of aluminum and coke, lending his help to coke oven inventor Heinrich Koppers, an innovator in transformation of industrial waste into usable products such as sulfur and coal gas.

In 1937, Mellon donated his substantial art collection and $10 million to establish the National Gallery of Art on the National Mall in Washington, D.C. He died on August 27 of that year.

George Westinghouse Jr.

A prolific inventor who built generators to harness the power of Niagara Falls, Westinghouse adopted Pittsburgh as his home in 1868. He formed the Westinghouse Electric Company, where his use of alternating current made electricity practical for lighting, transportation and power.

Westinghouse was born October 6, 1846, in Central Bridge, upstate New York. He patented his first invention, a rotary engine, at age 15.

Historians say his influence on industrial history and the nation's railroads is unmatched. His nearly 400 patents include the automatic railroad air brake, electrical transformers and automobile air shock absorbers.

The financial panic of 1907 caused Westinghouse, a conscientious employer who built a planned urban community for his workers, to lose control of his companies. He died on March 12, 1914.

Homestead Grays,
Champions of Homestead
& Vicinity, 1913.

1913: Cumberland Posey Jr. is seated in the second row, third from left.

Cumberland Posey Sr.

THE POSEYS

The life of Cumberland Posey Sr., known for most of his life as Commodore Posey, resembles the rags-to-riches story of Andrew Carnegie – with one exception. Posey was black. His success is remarkable in an era of stark segregation.

Posey worked his way up from riverboat pilot to owner of coal and steel companies along with some 42 steamboats. He was the city's first black millionaire.

Posey was born near Washington, D.C., in 1858. He moved to Homestead, the base of his business operations. He ran the area's largest black-owned business, the Diamond Coke and Coal Company. For 14 years, he was president of the Pittsburgh Courier, one of the nation's oldest and most influential black newspapers. Posey died in Homestead in 1926.

Posey's son, Cumberland Posey Jr., also was a successful businessman. He was a player, manager and owner of the fabled Homestead Grays.

The Grays, one of two Negro League baseball teams in Pittsburgh, was home to such greats as Josh Gibson, known as the "black Babe Ruth." Cumberland Posey was the Grays' principal owner from its founding in 1912 until his death in 1946.

c. 1934: Molten iron is poured from a ladle into molds inside a steel mill.

industry and steel

The backbreaking battles waged in "Victory Valley" – often by women, pensioners and boys as young as 16 – helped win wars in Europe and Asia.

More tons of steel passed through Pittsburgh's port during World War II than either the Panama or Suez canals; Ohio River shipyards held contracts for more than $1 billion in new landing craft and destroyers; factories created everything from barbed wire to armor-plated battleships.

Pittsburgh's steel industry had been building toward this climactic moment for more than a century, and it would be decimated within the second half of another.

Just as French and British armies in the 18th century had fought over the Point, where the Monongahela and Allegheny rivers form the Ohio, industrialists angled for space along the waterways during the Industrial Revolution.

Ironmaking had been important here since Colonial times, but Pittsburgh became the "Steel City" after industrialist Andrew Carnegie returned from a trip to England in 1873 determined to build an iron-to-steel converter, called a Bessemer furnace, since replaced by more efficient technologies.

From 1875 to 1980, the region served as the world's steel-making capital, pouring out the steel for such American icons as the Brooklyn Bridge and the Empire State Building.

With factories belching orange flames from towering furnaces, Pittsburgh drew immigrant workers from throughout the world: Ireland, Italy, Germany, Poland, Slovakia and Eastern Europe, chief among them.

Sons followed their fathers and grandfathers into the mills. Each job there generated dozens of manufacturing jobs. These paychecks sustained locally owned businesses.

By World War II, Pittsburgh was outfitting the Allied Forces. A $75 million expansion of United States Steel's Homestead Works in 1941 covered 120 acres. The mill's 12,000-ton press forged steel for countless battleships, including the *USS Missouri*, on whose decks the Japanese surrendered to end World War II.

1943: A worker sprays steel emerging from a 7,000-ton press at United States Steel's Homestead Works.

1952: The Jones & Laughlin Steel Corporation lights up the night sky over the Mon Valley. By 1894, J&L was out of the iron business and produced only steel. By the mid-20th century, J&L was one of the biggest steel producers in the world. It played a vital role in the defense industry during World War II. By the 1980s, as the steel industry here declined, J&L's vast plants along both sides of the Monongahela River closed.

c. 1910-20: A man stands between two machine-molded, staggered-tooth gears manufactured by the Mesta Machine Company in West Homestead. The plant covered more than 20 acres and employed about 3,000 people in the late 1910s. Mesta at the time was one of the world's leading manufacturers of machinery and equipment used to make steel. Products included gas and steam blowing engines for blast furnaces, forging presses, shears, cut and machine-molded gears and rolls for rolling mills. In 1959, Soviet Premier Nikita Khrushchev visited the plant as part of his American tour. In 1983, WHEMCO acquired Mesta's assets.

The Aluminum Cooking Utensil Company in New Kensington made cartridge cases, the Miller Printing Machine Company in Pittsburgh produced gun mounts, and Consolidated Lamp and Glass in Coraopolis turned out torpedo air flasks. Dravo Corporation on Neville Island and United States Steel's American Bridge Company in Ambridge became major builders of warships.

Big Steel continued in Pittsburgh through the post-war years, filling demands for cars, washing machines and building materials.

Then, in the mid-1980s, cheaper steel imports came into the country as Pittsburgh factories dealt with higher production costs.

In the past 30 years, Pittsburgh-area manufacturing jobs dropped by half to 144,847. Jobs in primary metals dropped by 70 percent over this period – but the number of service industry jobs increased by a third to 394,041.

Steel's collapse also drained the overall population. The Pittsburgh region lost 289,000 residents from 1970 to 1990.

By 1986, the once-massive Homestead Works was gone, cut into chunks of pricey scrap metal and fed into newer minimills as recycled material.

United States Steel uses part of the Homestead Works site for its Research and Technology Center to make small quantities of experimental steels.

NOTABLE BUSINESSES

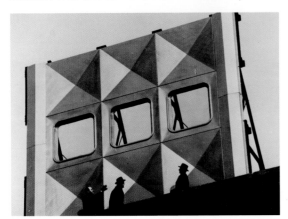

1913: The Gulf Oil Company opened the nation's first gas station in 1913 on Baum Boulevard in East Liberty.

1951: The Alcoa Building, a 30-story skyscraper Downtown, was constructed of prefabricated sheets of aluminum.

Alcoa Incorporated was founded in 1888 as the Pittsburgh Reduction Company to make aluminum and was renamed Aluminum Company of America. In 1999, the company officially became Alcoa Incorporated. The company's products were used in the Wright Brothers' airplane at Kitty Hawk in 1903 and the lunar space module in 1969. The company is now based in New York but maintains a corporate center on the North Side.

Consolidation Coal was formed in 1860 in Western Maryland, then merged with Pittsburgh Coal Company in 1945. It was acquired by Continental Oil Company and then by DuPont and Rheinbraun. In 2004, it went fully public and is known as Consol Energy Incorporated to reflect its diversification into other forms of energy. It is based in Upper Saint Clair.

Duquesne Light Company had its roots in the Allegheny County Light Company, founded in 1881 by entrepreneurs including George Westinghouse. It was one of the first electric companies in the country. The Philadelphia Company acquired Allegheny County Light. In 1912, Philadelphia Company bought the competing Duquesne Light Company and gave that name to the Allegheny County Light Company. A pioneer in nuclear power when it opened the Shippingport Atomic Power Station in 1958, Duquesne Light later became DQE, sold its nuclear plants and in 2007 merged with the Macquarie Consortium of Australia.

G.C. Murphy Company was founded in 1906 by George C. Murphy, a former McCrory's store manager, in McKeesport. The Murphy's chain grew to more than 500 stores offering dry goods and lunch counters. The company moved into the suburbs with its Murphy Marts. Those large stores were acquired in 1985 by Ames Department Stores Incorporated, eventually closing after Ames bought the Zayre's chain and later went out of business in 2002. Murphy's smaller five-and-dimes were bought by McCrory's.

Gulf Oil Corporation was founded in 1901, when the Mellon family invested in the Spindletop, Texas, oil gusher. The company was headquartered in Pittsburgh's Gulf Building, now Gulf Tower, an art deco skyscraper with a step-pyramid dome. A lantern on top indicates weather changes with colors. The company was acquired in 1984 by Chevron Incorporated. Its overseas interests are now owned by Hinduja Group, a private worldwide Indian business.

H.J. Heinz Company was founded in 1869 by Henry John Heinz, a young horseradish bottler who sold his products in clear glass bottles domestically and abroad well before 1900. Acquiring other companies quickened in the 1960s and continues to this day. The company's North Side plant still stands, one of 110 locations worldwide.

Joseph Horne Company was founded by young Bedford County native Joseph Horne in 1849 and moved to a location at Penn Avenue and Stanwix Street in 1922. It was known for its "carriage trade" among the well-to-do and its Christmas tree display on its corner façade. After a series of acquisitions, Joseph Horne became Lazarus stores in 1994. In 2003, the merged Federated-Macy's chain took over.

c. 1900: The main entrance to the H.J. Heinz Company plant on the North Side.

J.R. Weldin Company, a Wood Street stationer founded in 1852, is still operating more than 150 years later, offering office supplies, maps, stationery and leather goods.

Kaufmann's was a dry goods store opened by Jacob and Isaac Kaufmann in 1871. The store grew to a regional department store chain with a block-long flagship store on Smithfield Street, famous for its ornate corner clock. The chain was eventually bought by the May Company, which closed the company headquarters in Pittsburgh in 2002. May was bought by Federated Department Stores in 2005. The Kaufmann's name was retired in 2006 when Federated converted the former May-owned stores to Macy's stores.

Mellon Bank was opened in 1869 as T. Mellon & Sons by Thomas Mellon after his 10-year term as an Allegheny County Common Pleas judge. Sons Andrew W. and Richard B. Mellon grew the bank into one of the nation's largest, having merged it in 1946 with Union Trust, which the Mellon family also controlled. In 2007, Mellon merged with the Bank of New York to form Bank of New York Mellon Corporation.

McCrory's was founded in 1882 in Scottdale by John G. McCrory, who noted the success of Woolworth's. The corporation operated five-and-dime stores under several names, including McLellan, H.L. Green and TG&Y and even took over G.C. Murphy's smaller stores before filing for bankruptcy in 2001.

Mine Safety Appliances Company was founded in 1914 by members of Pittsburgh's Dieke family to provide safety helmets and lamps for coal miners. During World War II, general manager John Ryan Jr. spearheaded efforts to concentrate on safety equipment for non-mining industries, including firefighting and military uses. His son was named CEO in 1997.

PPG Industries Incorporated was established by John B. Ford and John Pitcairn in 1883 as Pittsburgh Plate Glass Company. PPG acquired paint and chemical companies and began producing glass for the new automotive and aviation industries, as well as a post-World War II housing boom.

United States Steel Corporation was organized in 1901, when Elbert H. Gary and J.P. Morgan headed a group that bought Carnegie Steel Company and combined it with Federal Steel Company and five other companies. The resulting corporation was the first billion-dollar company. After becoming USX in 1986, to reflect its diversified portfolio, the corporation reorganized in 2001 and spun off its steel and steel-related businesses. In 2002 it again became United States Steel Corporation, today employing 49,000 worldwide.

Westinghouse Air Brake Company supplied railroad products worldwide after George Westinghouse invented the air brake, which increased rail safety by allowing the engineer to have control over a train's brake system. Westinghouse in 1869 established the company, which exists as the reorganized Wabtec Corporation. Wabtec is headquartered in Wilmerding, employs 6,000 on five continents and produces a broad range of products for the rail and transit industries.

Westinghouse Electric Corporation was founded in 1886 by George Westinghouse, who won the "War of Currents" against Thomas Edison. Westinghouse's use of alternating current was accepted over direct current. The company produced the first commercial radio broadcast at KDKA. The company also produced electric appliances for households and technologies for industries and government. In the 1970s, the corporation began selling off some units. The corporation survives today as the builder of nuclear power plants around the world.

WQED became the country's first community television station in 1954, after children raised funds to get the station on the air. With support from the A.W. Mellon Trust, the Ford Foundation and the Arbuckle-Jamison Foundation and a deed to property in Oakland from Pittsburgh Plate Glass Company, the station has provided award-winning programs, including the iconic "Mister Rogers' Neighborhood."

CLYDE HARE/CARNEGIE LIBRARY OF PITTSBURGH

1950: "Meet me under the Kaufmann's clock" is all Pittsburghers needed to say to connect with friends and colleagues Downtown. The store has been transformed into a Macy's but the clock remains as an enduring landmark.

CARNEGIE LIBRARY OF PITTSBURGH

In the days before "Mister Rogers' Neighborhood" became famous as one of WQED-TV's premiere shows, there were several well-known programs for children. Among them was "Charming Children," shown here during filming.

LOU MALKIN/CARNEGIE LIBRARY OF PITTSBURGH

1974: G.C. Murphy Company, Downtown

1946: Workers at Westinghouse Electric Corporation's East Pittsburgh Works vote to return to work. The vote was conducted at Turtle Creek Stadium on Lynn Avenue in Turtle Creek.

ORGANIZED LABOR

It began with the 1814 strike of Pittsburgh's shoemakers.

Pennsylvania authorities brought the shoemakers, called "cordwainers," to trial in 1815 for conspiring to form a syndicate of workers who would hold out for better wages and working conditions. Like a similar trial in Philadelphia, the judge determined that collective bargaining, forming unions and speaking as a united voice to management added up to an unlawful restraint of trade.

Despite the legal setback, workers would continue to battle owners and state and federal government for the right to collectively organize and fight for higher wages, better conditions and a fair shake from management.

Much of the labor movement was born in Pittsburgh. From 1845 to 1848, Pittsburgh's women textile laborers struck to get a 10-hour day. In 1865, after an eight-month strike, the first trade union agreement in America was made in Pittsburgh between the Sons of Vulcan and the iron industry. The bloodiest riot in Pittsburgh history – the 1877 railroad strike – lasted four days and left 45 people dead.

For the next six decades, unions won some battles – Slavic butchers beat management in the 1909 McKees Rocks industrial slaughterhouse strike; the American Federation of Labor held its founding meeting in Pittsburgh in 1881 – and lost others, like the bloody Homestead Strike of 1892.

After a Democratic Party sweep in 1936, federal reforms spurred labor organizing and made what the cordwainers did in 1814 completely legal. That led the same types of laborers who failed during the Homestead strike to form legally the Steel Workers Organizing Committee. Today, that's the United Steelworkers –- headquartered in Pittsburgh, the continent's largest trade union representing nearly 1.2 million laborers in a wide range of crafts.

The Congress of Industrial Organizations conducted its founding convention in Pittsburgh in 1938. The AFL and CIO would merge in 1955, creating a federation representing an estimated 15 million members.

UNION SWITCH & SIGNAL, ARCHIVES SERVICES CENTER, UNIVERSITY OF PITTSBURGH

1914: Women carrying signs and flags march on Edgewood Avenue in Swissvale. Women played a vital role in the 1914 strike by Westinghouse workers. The strike at Union Switch & Signal, founded by George Westinghouse, began June 12 when 1,100 to 1,400 people walked off the job at lunchtime. Organized by the Allegheny Congenial Industrial Union, the strikers demanded an eight-hour day, reinstatement of discharged union men, permission for workmen to enact grievance committees and higher pay for holidays and overtime.

Railroad strike

On July 21, 1877, militia called up from Philadelphia shot into striking workers, who had swarmed the Pennsylvania Railroad yard in the Strip District. Twenty people were killed, including a woman and three children. Iron workers joined the enraged crowd, which swelled to 20,000 and forced the militia to take cover in the rail yard's sturdy roundhouse. The mob set it on fire, and in the retreat, say some accounts, another 20 rioters and five guardsmen were killed.

Looters torched 39 buildings in the rail yard, more than 100 locomotives and more than 500 railcars. A bigger show of force stopped the uprising, but not before it had spread to Chicago, St. Louis and other cities.

The Homestead strike

When falling steel prices ate into profits, Andrew Carnegie and his business partner, Henry Clay Frick, demanded workers at Carnegie's Homestead Works choose between their jobs and the union, which had been seeking a new contract. The workers chose the union, and the owners closed the plant.

Hoping to end the standoff, Frick on June 6, 1892, sent 300 Pinkerton guards by barge to confront the workers, leading to a gun battle that left seven workers and three guards dead. The Pinkertons eventually surrendered, and company officials negotiated with town leaders for their release. A week later, the state militia arrived in Homestead to restore order.

The holdout between the owners and employees continued until November, when the workers asked to come back. That capitulation effectively ended organizing attempts until the 1930s.

THE COURIER

Edwin Harleston, a security guard at the H.J. Heinz Company plant, had a dream. He wanted to write.

He established a newspaper in 1907 that would grow into the largest, and one of most influential, black newspapers in the country. Almost from that first day, the Pittsburgh Courier was at the center of a long and hard struggle for equality and against discrimination.

It gained national prominence after attorney Robert Lee Vann became editor and publisher, treasurer and legal counsel in 1910. Vann guided it to a circulation of 250,000 and more than 400 employees in 14 cities. A network of Pullman porters, who worked for the railroads, helped distribute the newspaper.

In the 1920s, the newspaper was a staunch advocate for anti-lynching legislation, measures that were invariably obstructed by Southern politicians in Congress.

Sportswriter Wendell Smith denounced segregation in the major leagues and championed the career of Jackie Robinson. Smith's own career took him from Pittsburgh to Chicago. He is included in a special exhibit at the National Baseball Hall of Fame & Museum in Cooperstown, New York, honoring top baseball writers and broadcasters.

In the 1932 election, Vann, a one-time Republican, urged black voters to turn away from the party of Lincoln to support Franklin D. Roosevelt. During World War II, the paper designed a "double V" campaign – victory at home, victory abroad.

The Courier was acquired in 1966 by John H. Sengstacke and reorganized as the New Pittsburgh Courier.

Press operators adjust feed paper on rollers in the home offices of the Pittsburgh Courier. One of the oldest and most prestigious black newspapers in the United States, the weekly newspaper's staff included many skilled technicians in its printing operations.

PIONEERS

Nellie Bly

Elizabeth Cochrane, a journalist better known as Nellie Bly, was born on May 5, 1864, in Cochran's Mills. She began her career at age 18 as a feature writer for The Pittsburgh Dispatch. Bly joined the New York World in 1887, where she feigned insanity to get into the Women's Lunatic Asylum on Blackwell's Island. Her story brought needed reforms. On November 14, 1889, she set sail on a trip around the world, aiming to beat the record of Phileas Fogg, a fictional character in Jules Verne's "Around the World in 80 Days." It took her 72 days, 6 hours, 11 minutes and 14 seconds to complete the journey. She died January 27, 1922, in New York.

Hugh Henry Brackenridge

Born in Scotland in 1748, Brackenridge came to Pittsburgh to practice law after graduation from what is now Princeton University. He was elected to the Pennsylvania Legislature in 1786 and championed creation of Allegheny County. He sponsored the bill that established what is now the University of Pittsburgh. He established the Pittsburgh Gazette, the first newspaper published west of the Alleghenies, acted as a mediator in the Whiskey Rebellion of 1794 and served as a justice on the state Supreme Court. He died on June 25, 1816, in Carlisle.

Rachel Carson

An author and scientist born on May 27, 1907, in Springdale, Carson is best known for writing "Silent Spring" in 1962. The book warned the public about the long-term effects of misusing pesticides and created a worldwide awareness of the dangers of environmental pollution. She died of cancer on April 14, 1964, in Silver Spring, Maryland. The Ninth Street Bridge linking Downtown and the North Side has been renamed in her honor.

Martin Robinson Delaney

A physician and champion of civil rights, Delaney published a black newspaper, The Mystery, in Pittsburgh. He was born May 6, 1812, in Charles Town, in what is now West Virginia. He also was editor of Frederick Douglass' North Star from 1847 to 1849. During the Civil War, he was the first black American to be appointed to the rank of major in the Army. He died January 24, 1885, in Wilberforce, Ohio.

Daisy Lampkin

Born in Reading in 1888, Lampkin came to Pittsburgh in 1909 and became a national leader in the women's suffrage and the civil rights movements. An expert fundraiser, she was vice president of the Pittsburgh Courier for 36 years and was on the executive board of the National Council of Negro Women. She became national field secretary for the National Association for the Advancement of Colored People in 1935 and held the post until her health began to fail in 1947. Lampkin is the first black woman honored with a Pennsylvania historical marker, which stands outside the Webster Avenue home she shared with her husband, William, until her death on March 10, 1965, at age 76.

Judith Resnick

A National Aeronautics and Space Administration astronaut, Resnick died aboard the space shuttle Challenger when it exploded after launch on January 28, 1986. She earned a bachelor's degree in electrical engineering from Carnegie Mellon University and was posthumously awarded the Congressional Space Medal of Honor. She was born on April 5, 1949, in Akron, Ohio.

Jane Grey Swisshelm

A women's rights activist and abolitionist, Swisshelm was born on December 6, 1815, in Pittsburgh. She started an abolitionist newspaper in Pittsburgh in 1848 and became the first female salaried newspaper writer and editor in the city. She published an autobiography, "Half a Century," in 1880 and continued writing for various publications, including Horace Greeley's New York Tribune, until her death in Swissvale on July 22, 1884.

KEITH HODAN/TRIBUNE-REVIEW

George Zambelli Sr.

Zambelli headed New Castle-based Zambelli Fireworks Internationale from 1957 until his death on Christmas Day, 2003, in Pittsburgh. The company puts on 3,500 fireworks shows every year, including one at Pittsburgh's Fourth of July celebration. Its displays have entertained every president since John F. Kennedy. Born in New Castle in 1924, he regarded himself as an artist, painting the sky with colors.

INVENTORS

John Brashear

Born in Brownsville on November 24, 1840, Brashear invented a method of coating telescope lenses that vastly improved their range. He set up a shop on the North Side, and large observatories worldwide soon used Brashear's discovery. He was known lovingly throughout Pittsburgh as "Uncle John" and helped plan the Carnegie Technical Schools, now Carnegie Mellon University. He also spearheaded the building of the Allegheny Observatory, which moved from Perrysville Avenue to Riverview Park in 1912. He died in Pittsburgh on April 7, 1920.

Frank Conrad

Conrad installed a radio transmitter in his garage as far back as 1916 that evolved from station 8XK into the world's first commercial radio station, KDKA. Born on May 4, 1874, in Pittsburgh, he held patents for more than 200 inventions, ranging from electric clocks to applications used in automobile lighting and ignition. He began as a mechanical assembler with the Westinghouse Electric & Manufacturing Company in 1890 at the age of 16 and rose to chief assistant engineer. He died on December 10, 1941, in Miami.

George Ferris

Ferris, born February 14, 1859, in Galesburg, Illinois, brought amazement and delight to the world with the Ferris Wheel. During the 1880s, he founded G.W.G. Ferris & Company in Pittsburgh, where he tested metals for railroad and bridge construction. The Ferris Wheel debuted at the World's Columbian Exhibition in Chicago in 1893 with some parts that came from Pittsburgh. The 250-foot rotating wheel, which carried 1,400 passengers at a time, became a sensation. Ferris became embroiled in a lawsuit alleging he had copied the wheel's design from other sources. Ferris ultimately owed money as a result of a patent infringement. Soon after, his wife left him. He died in Mercy Hospital in 1896 at the age of 37.

Robert Fulton

In 1810, Fulton built in Pittsburgh the first steamboat that floated down the western rivers. The boat was named the *New Orleans*. It, and others like it, revolutionized transportation and shipping in the nation. Fulton was born in Lancaster County in 1765 and died February 24, 1815, in New York City.

1807: Fulton's first boat, the *Clermont*, is known as the first commercially successful steamboat. In the hull, he placed the engine, and on each side, a primitive paddle wheel. It left New York City and traveled against the Hudson current at an average of five miles an hour, arriving in Albany, New York, 32 hours later.

Samuel Langley

Born August 22, 1834, in Roxbury, Massachusetts, Langley's work making telescopes brought him to Allegheny Observatory in 1867 as director and professor of astrophysics at what is now the University of Pittsburgh. There was no such thing as standard time then. Langley used a telescope to obtain accurate time from the position of the stars. More than 40 railroads subscribed to this service, and the money helped finance the observatory. In 1887, he became secretary of the Smithsonian Institution, continuing efforts to develop a flying machine. On December 8, 1903, his "Great Aerodrome" fell into the Potomac River, just days before the Wright Brothers' successful flight at Kitty Hawk, North Carolina. Langley died in Aiken, South Carolina on February 27, 1906. Pitt's Langley Hall is named for him.

William Hunter Dammond

William Hunter Dammond was the first black student to graduate from what is now the University of Pittsburgh, receiving a civil engineering degree with honors in 1893.

Born in the lower Hill District in 1873, he made his mark as a professor, mathematician and inventor. He designed patented systems that increased rail safety by signaling the engineer whether the rail ahead was occupied. One of these systems, the Dammond Circuit, used alternating current and was developed while he worked in Great Britain from 1910 to 1916.

Versions of the Dammond Circuit were used on subways in New York City and on railroads in Pennsylvania, Long Island and New York. Despite his patents, Dammond had to fight for recognition of his innovations.

He died in 1956.

LIBRARY OF CONGRESS

George Westinghouse Bridge, spanning Turtle Creek at Lincoln Highway.

George Richardson

There'd be no such thing as the Parkway if it weren't for Richardson.

As engineer for the Allegheny County Authority, he spearheaded the design of the Penn-Lincoln Parkway, the Fort Pitt Bridge and the Fort Duquesne Bridge. He also designed the George Westinghouse Bridge with five concrete arches over the Turtle Creek Valley. Born in Colorado in 1896, Richardson came to the area in 1920 with a degree in engineering from the University of Colorado. He joined American Bridge Company, then based in Ambridge, as a draftsman. He started his own firm in 1939. He died in Pittsburgh in 1988.

CARNEGIE LIBRARY OF PITTSBURGH

c. 1894: Smithfield Street Bridge.

John Roebling

Roebling revolutionized industry by introducing a process using rope made from wire. Stronger and more flexible, it soon revolutionized bridge building. He was born in Prussia on June 12, 1806, and was 25 when he came to Western Pennsylvania. After the Great Fire of 1845, Roebling used this rope to rebuild the Monongahela Bridge, where the Smithfield Street Bridge stands today. In the 1850s, he built a wire rope suspension bridge that was a forerunner to the present-day Roberto Clemente Bridge. He died on July 22, 1869, from tetanus while crafting his masterpiece, the Brooklyn Bridge in New York City.

immigration and growth

In and around Fort Pitt, the city's first immigrants – English and Scots-Irish, primarily – built a last stop for early American explorers. Swedes, French and others passed through. A handful of German Protestants stayed, laying a foundation for future generations of their countrymen. Small numbers of black settlers – free and enslaved – labored here, on the fringe of the United States.

The first Pittsburghers worked mostly to serve themselves, manufacturing clothing and other necessary goods. The first United States Census in 1790 recorded 1,853 people – 40 of them slaves.

By 1810, hints of Pittsburgh's future emerged. That year, two blast furnaces and four air furnaces refined 400 tons of metal. New industry beckoned new immigrants, who still came primarily from the British Isles – Ireland as well – to practice the metalworking craft passed from father to son since the Middle Ages.

It was an artisan's work. Puddlers, as they were known, watched the molten metal carefully, seeking subtle signs of what to add and when to finish. The young country's most plentiful coal fields and the transportation offered by the rivers made this place as close to ideal as a puddler could hope.

c. 1930: Animals await their fate along Logan Street in the Hill District, where signs in the window of Caplan's Market offer roasts, pig heads and pure lard. It was a time when many small grocery stores existed in Pittsburgh's neighborhoods.

Irish Catholics, pushed by famine and discrimination, were drawn by frontier jobs and land. They swelled the young city's ranks. Finding discrimination here as well, they formed some of the city's earliest parochial schools.

By 1850, Pittsburgh would be home to more than 46,000 people. Laborers cut into lush forests, and Western European boat-builders shaped the wood. Pittsburgh timber was solid. When settlers arrived at their destinations, they tore the boats apart, desperate for material strong enough to make a home. In historic districts from New Orleans to Memphis, wood is hidden beneath layers of paint that was pulled from Pittsburgh's forests.

The Steel City began emerging in earnest in the 1880s. Massive Bessemer converters required no artistry to make steel – just a broad back and an unshakable work ethic. Eastern Europeans answered the call, with Poles, Slovaks, Russians and Germans flocking to the mills. Steel magnates sent emissaries to Italian villages, promising jobs, and the Italians joined the wave. From the South came black men, women and children fleeing the darkness of Jim Crow.

Pittsburgh and the city of Allegheny, now the North Side, began growing at the rate of about 100,000 people every 10 years. By 1930, more than 100,000 of Pittsburgh's 670,000 people were born in another country. Thirty thousand came from Poland and Germany.

Immigration peaked after Congress passed the Johnson-Reed Act of 1924, which set quotas of foreigners allowed into the United States. By the 1970s, the city's ethnic enclaves started breaking up as people moved to the suburbs. After mill jobs disappeared in the 1980s, Pittsburgh lost more than half of its population.

As the city turns 250, new immigrants are few. Hispanic immigration seen elsewhere in the country largely bypassed Pittsburgh. Instead, the newest residents come from India, China and other parts of Asia. They are medical researchers, physicians, computer programmers and high-tech manufacturers. They find work in the city's universities, hospitals and laboratories, drawn by Pittsburgh's newest and oldest industry: possibility.

THE PITTSBURGH SURVEY

Long before Pittsburgh was a hotbed of scientific innovation, the city was the subject of one of the most ambitious research projects ever undertaken in the United States. Funded by the widow of wealthy New York financier Russell Sage, 70 sociologists descended here in 1907 to interview workers, investigate daily life in slums and mill towns and document it with photographs. First published in Collier's and later collected in six volumes, the Pittsburgh Survey and its stark portrayal of urban squalor became a foundation for economic and social reform.

LEWIS W. HINE/CARNEGIE LIBRARY OF PITTSBURGH

1908: Russian immigrants crowded into tenements at Homestead Court while seeking employment in the steel mills. Common language and culture clustered newcomers into neighborhoods that still retain their ethnic flavor.

ALLEGHENY CITY

A century ago, Western Pennsylvania's sister cities of Pittsburgh and Allegheny were locked in a bitter battle that would profoundly alter the region's future.

After decades of pushing to grow beyond the Monongahela and Allegheny rivers, Pittsburgh – the state's second-largest city after Philadelphia – saw a chance to become a metropolis near the top rung of great American cities.

Allegheny – then the third-largest municipality, situated north of Pittsburgh on the banks of the Allegheny and Ohio rivers – found itself in a struggle for survival. At stake: identity and autonomy after nearly a century of development on its own.

It was one of the most controversial annexations in United States history. Voters flocked to polls June 12, 1906 – many wearing pins proclaiming "Yes" or buttons defiantly answering "No."

Annexation fever was gripping other cities, including New York and Boston, in the late 19th and early 20th centuries. It was considered part of a progressive movement to bring reforms to urban life. Allegheny, too, was annexing its smaller neighbors.

Allegheny was incorporated as a borough with about 1,000 residents in 1828, and became a city in 1840. Allegheny City contained a sprawling park and key railroad and water transportation links. It was home to a diverse community of business and manufacturing. For recreation, people flocked to Exposition Park, home of baseball's first World Series between the Pittsburgh Pirates and the Boston American League Baseball Club –

1905: The Allegheny branch of the Carnegie Library was built in 1890. and provided books and resources for residents of the North Side until lightning damaged the roof in 2006.

now the Red Sox – in 1903. The city also had the original Phipps Conservatory, a gift of Henry Phipps, a partner of Andrew Carnegie's.

H.J. Heinz, the food-processing tycoon whose plant was located in Allegheny City, spoke in favor of consolidation at a rally attended by an estimated 4,000 people. "Let us stand before the world as we are, a great municipality, instead of an aggregation of villages," Heinz said in news accounts of the time.

"The desire of Pittsburgh for its annexation was now a mania," wrote local historian Charles W. Dahlinger, who witnessed the political battle, in his 1918 history, "Old Allegheny."

On the other hand, "Allegheny was proud of her existence, and her death struggles were severe," he wrote.

Pittsburgh had been trying to annex Allegheny City, along with neighborhoods in the South Side and East End, for nearly 70 years.

But in early 1906, the rules changed. State legislators quietly hurried a consolidation bill through, with the blessings of Governor Samuel W. Pennypacker, a reform advocate.

Before, Allegheny City's fate was tied to what a majority of its residents wanted. The Greater Pittsburgh Act of 1906 authorized a referendum that would count the total votes for and against annexation in Pittsburgh and Allegheny as a whole, with an overall majority settling the issue.

Allegheny City – at 150,000 people, half of Pittsburgh's population – essentially lost the day Pennypacker signed the bill.

The referendum carried even though nearly two out of three Allegheny residents opposed it.

The United States Supreme Court on November 18, 1907, upheld the Greater Pittsburgh Act as a legal annexation.

Pittsburgh officially annexed Allegheny City on December 7, 1907, and it became the North Side.

NEIGHBORHOODS

PUSHING THE BOUNDARIES

In 1787, Pittsburgh ended at Grant Street and what now is 11th Street. Pittsburgh expanded its borders through annexation. Many of its neighborhoods were once independent villages and towns.

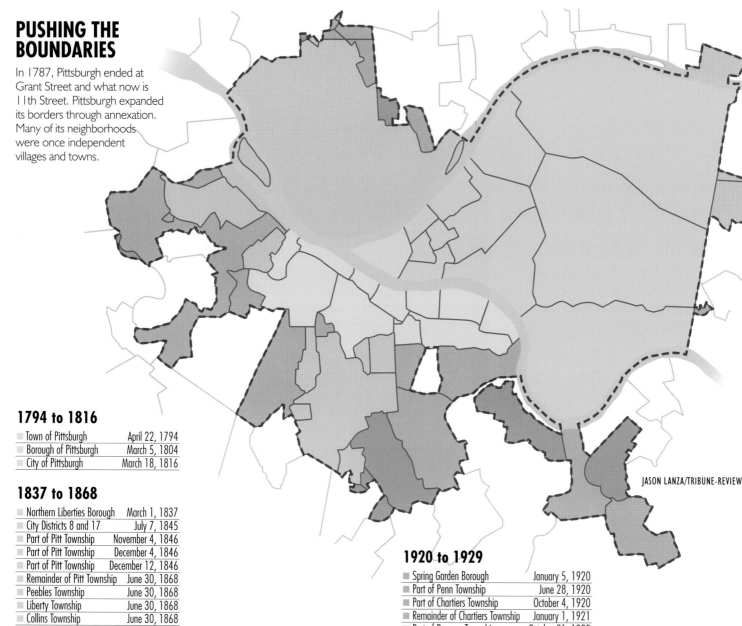

JASON LANZA/TRIBUNE-REVIEW

1794 to 1816

Town of Pittsburgh	April 22, 1794
Borough of Pittsburgh	March 5, 1804
City of Pittsburgh	March 18, 1816

1837 to 1868

Northern Liberties Borough	March 1, 1837
City Districts 8 and 17	July 7, 1845
Part of Pitt Township	November 4, 1846
Part of Pitt Township	December 4, 1846
Part of Pitt Township	December 12, 1846
Remainder of Pitt Township	June 30, 1868
Peebles Township	June 30, 1868
Liberty Township	June 30, 1868
Collins Township	June 30, 1868
Oakland Township	June 30, 1868
Lawrenceville Borough	June 30, 1868

1872

Union Borough	April 2, 1872
Temperanceville Borough	April 2, 1872
Mount Washington Borough	April 2, 1872
West Pittsburgh Borough	April 2, 1872
Monongahela Borough	April 2, 1872
South Pittsburgh Borough	April 2, 1872
Allentown Borough	April 2, 1872
Birmingham Borough	April 2, 1872
East Birmingham Borough	April 2, 1872
Saint Clair Borough	April 2, 1872
Ormsby Borough	April 2, 1872

1894 to 1916

Brushton Borough	December 1, 1894
Beltzhoover Borough	March 1, 1898
Elliott Borough	January 2, 1905
Esplen Borough	January 8, 1906
Sterrett Township	January 8, 1906
Montooth Borough	January 7, 1907
Sheraden Borough	November 21, 1907
City of Allegheny	December 7, 1907
West Liberty Borough	January 6, 1908
O'Hara Township	October 30, 1908
Beechview Borough	January 4, 1909
Part of Union Township	January 4 1909
Part of Baldwin Township	January 1, 1912
Part of Ross Township	December 19, 1916

1920 to 1929

Spring Garden Borough	January 5, 1920
Part of Penn Township	June 28, 1920
Part of Chartiers Township	October 4, 1920
Remainder of Chartiers Township	January 1, 1921
Part of Reserve Township	October 31, 1922
Saint Clair Borough	January 1, 1923
Parts of Lower Saint Clair Township	February 7, 1924
Part of Swissvale Borough	November 27, 1925
Carrick Borough	January 3, 1927
Knoxville Borough	January 3, 1927
Westwood Borough	January 3, 1927
Union Township	January 2, 1928
Part of Ross Township	June 29, 1928
Hays Borough	January 7, 1929
Part of Mifflin Township	February 15, 1929
Part of Ross Township	April 22, 1929
Part of Ross Township	April 25, 1929
Part of Ross Township	June 3, 1929
Part of Ross Township	July 1, 1929
Part of Mifflin Township	July 22, 1929

1930 to 1955

Part of Penn Township	January 2, 1930
Part of Penn Township	January 22, 1930
Overbrook Borough	January 6, 1930
Part of Baldwin Township	January 5, 1931
Part of Mifflin Township	February 27, 1931
Part of Reserve Township	March 20, 1931
Part of Baldwin Township	December 1, 1947
Part of Ross Township	April 28, 1948
Part of Baldwin Township	February 5, 1951
Part of Baldwin Township	March 13, 1951
Part of Robinson Township	August 19, 1955

ETHNIC NEIGHBORHOODS

Whether perched atop hills or reflecting Pittsburgh's industrial past, each of the city's 89 neighborhoods has a distinct character, created in part by the ethnic groups that settled there. Over the years, groups moved in and moved on. Here's a look at how these neighborhoods evolved:

September 30, 2006: The city's Bloomfield neighborhood is dubbed Pittsburgh's "Little Italy." Each year the neighborhood holds a festival featuring Italian food and games like bocce.

ANDREW RUSSELL/TRIBUNE-REVIEW

Bloomfield

Settled in early 1800s by John C. Winebiddle, who sold land to fellow German immigrants. An influx of Italian immigrants after World War I helped forge what is now known as Pittsburgh's "Little Italy."

Deutschtown

Settled by German and later Croatian immigrants, beginning in 1850 as Allegheny City spread east.

East Liberty

Home in the second half of the 19th century to such elite Pittsburgh families as the Mellons and Larimers. Urban renewal efforts in the 1960s destroyed much of the struggling economic base. The neighborhood has seen some success in revitalizing its shopping district.

Hazelwood

Settled by Scottish immigrants around 1784. The opening of Jones & Laughlin's steel plant in 1884 attracted Hungarian, Slovak, Polish and Irish immigrants.

Mount Washington/ Duquesne Heights

Known as Coal Hill prior to 1851, when German and Italian immigrant millworkers began settling here.

July 30, 2005: Mount Washington is famous for the view of Downtown from Grandview Avenue. The street is lined with restaurants, apartments and scenic lookouts.

KEITH HODAN/TRIBUNE-REVIEW

43

Hill District

Developed in the late 1850s by banker Thomas Mellon. Prosperous trolley-commuting residents were later replaced by Jewish immigrants and those from Wales, Italy, Syria, Greece, Poland and Russia. Blacks residents began arriving from the South around 1890 and are the predominant group today. The Hill District is the setting for a series of plays by Pulitzer Prize-winning playwright August Wilson.

Lawrenceville

Settled by composer Stephen Foster's family in 1814, immigrants from Germany, Ireland, Poland, Serbia and Croatia came to work the mills beginning in the mid-1800s.

North Side

First settled by Europeans in 1787, established as Allegheny City in 1840, it was home to German, English, Scottish, Irish and Eastern European immigrants. These groups maintain a presence. The neighborhood also has a strong black community.

Oakland

Settled by residents fleeing devastated Downtown after the Great Fire of 1845. The University of Pittsburgh moved here from Allegheny City in 1907. Pitt and other nearby universities have made it home to students and young families from around the world.

JOE APPEL/TRIBUNE-REVIEW

February 9, 2007: Pittsburgh's neighborhoods are dotted with community parks. With the city skyline in the background, youths play hockey on a frozen Lake Elizabeth in the North Side's West Park.

April 7, 2007: Pittsburgh's neighborhoods are steeped in their religious faith and its traditions. At the Immaculate Heart of Mary Church in Polish Hill, baskets of food are blessed on Holy Saturday.

Polish Hill

In 1885 Polish immigrants began settling there. It remains home to many of their descendants and the opulent Immaculate Heart of Mary Church.

South Side

Part of a 1763 British land grant, it was annexed by Pittsburgh in 1872. German, Irish, Polish, Lithuanian, Ukrainian and other Slavic immigrant workers settled there in the late 1800s, drawn by steel and glass manufacturing along the Monongahela River.

Strip District

Divided into lots in 1814, German, Irish and Polish immigrants settled in the next few decades to work in the foundries and glass factories. High-end loft apartments mark the resurgence of the Strip as a residential area.

Squirrel Hill

Jews from the Hill District and abroad began relocating to this then-rural area after Murray Avenue was paved in 1920. It is still a center for Pittsburgh's Jewish community, including immigrants from Israel and Eastern Europe.

June 7, 2002: The strip district is Pittsburgh's market basket. Stores along Penn Avenue and Smallman Street feature fresh seafood, vegetables, fruits and ethnic delights.

Rodef Shalom Congregation

1936: Trinity Episcopal Church

Saint Paul Cathedral

HOUSES OF WORSHIP

Religion played an important role on the frontier. After the French took possession of the Point on April 17, 1754, Father Denis Baron, a chaplain of the French army, celebrated Mass. Among the first institutions settlers established here were places of worship. These are among the earliest:

First Presbyterian Church of Pittsburgh

The roots of this church can be traced to 1758, when the British defeated the French at Fort Duquesne. A service of thanksgiving was conducted by Charles Beatty, a Presbyterian minister who was chaplain to General John Forbes. Heirs of William Penn donated land, originally used as an Indian burial ground, to the church, which was incorporated on September 29, 1787, by an act of the Pennsylvania Legislature. The present-day church on Sixth Avenue, Downtown, was dedicated in 1905.

Smithfield United Church of Christ

Mainly German immigrants built a one-room, log meeting house in 1783 at the intersection of Diamond Alley, now Forbes Avenue, and Wood Street, making it the city's oldest church. The heirs of William Penn also gave the congregation land in 1787 for a new church on Smithfield Street. In 1812, the church was named the German Evangelical Protestant Church. It is now Smithfield United Church of Christ.

Trinity Episcopal Cathedral

Trustees involved in the church received a grant from the Penn family in 1787 for land the French, British and Native Americans used as a burial ground. The church got its charter in 1805, and the first church building was octagonal, earning it the name "The Round Church," built where the Wood Street subway station is now. The present church, built on Sixth Avenue, Downtown, in 1872, became Trinity Cathedral in 1927. Eighteenth-century graves rest in the churchyard.

Saint Patrick

Saint Patrick was the first Catholic parish in Pittsburgh, established in 1808, predating the Diocese of Pittsburgh by 35 years. The first church was built on 11th Street and dedicated three years later. The church has been rebuilt three times, twice because of fire. It is now located at 17th Street and Liberty Avenue and is part of Saint Patrick-Saint Stanislaus Kostka Parish in the Strip District.

Saint Paul Cathedral

The first Saint Paul Church was constructed at Grant Street and Fifth Avenue, Downtown, and was consecrated as a cathedral in 1843. It burned to the ground eight years later. Church officials suspected arson because of opposition to the large number of Roman Catholic immigrants entering the country from Ireland, Germany and Italy. A second cathedral was built on the same site in 1855. The land was sold to Henry Clay Frick, and the current cathedral was built on Fifth Avenue in Oakland. It opened in 1906.

Bethel African Methodist Episcopal Church

Bethel AME Church is the oldest black church and the first African Methodist church west of the Allegheny Mountains. It was founded in 1808 in a home on Front Street and known simply as the "African Church." Bethel started the area's first school for black children in 1831 and was host for the state's first civil rights convention in 1841. It served as a station in the Underground Railroad. It is now located on Webster Avenue in the Hill District.

Rodef Shalom Congregation

Rodef Shalom was chartered by the Commonwealth in 1856, though its roots go back to 1840. It is the oldest Jewish congregation in Western Pennsylvania. When founded, it was mostly made up of German Jews. It grew as Eastern European Jews joined the congregation. The first two temples were built on Eighth Street, formerly Hancock Street, Downtown. The current temple on Fifth Avenue in Oakland was completed in 1907.

CARNEGIE LIBRARY OF PITTSBURGH

First Presbyterian Church

BLAIR/CARNEGIE LIBRARY OF PITTSBURGH

1953: Smithfield United Church of Christ

March 6, 1946: A fire that started in a building supply store on Liberty Avenue spread to the nearby Pittsburgh and West Virginia Railroad trestle and the two-block-long Wabash Terminal on Ferry Street, now Stanwix Street. The destruction opened the way for development of the Golden Triangle.

renaissance

Living up to its reputation as "hell with the lid taken off," Pittsburgh found new life from a devastating fire on March 6, 1946.

Flames engulfed a sprawling, dilapidated railroad warehouse district near the Point. Mayor David L. Lawrence had grown up there in an Irish immigrant neighborhood amid the factories. He and other leaders realized immediately the blaze would help them remake Pittsburgh.

Quicker than it ramped up for war production in 1941, Pittsburgh's steel industry jerked to an abrupt slowdown with the end of World War II. Lawrence and Pittsburgh financier Richard King Mellon saw that the city could move forward only by branching out beyond heavy industry. Together, they pushed forward the city's first "Renaissance," a period of civic, economic and environmental renewal that lasted through the 1960s.

Public and private leaders, working through the newly formed Allegheny Conference on Community Development, pushed through major changes in the quality of the local environment and the physical look of the city. The conference supported phased-in smoke controls, educated the public on the need for cleaner air and lobbied for an Allegheny County anti-pollution law in 1949.

Meanwhile, several landmark projects grew out of the period, including Point State Park; Gateway Center; the Civic Arena, later Mellon Arena; the United States Steel Tower and the Penn-Lincoln Parkway.

Starting in 1977 and lasting through the 1980s, Renaissance II brought a second building boom that included the construction of One Oxford Centre in 1983, PPG Place in 1984 and Fifth Avenue Place in 1988.

Some have argued that a period of building in the early 21st century, including publicly financed projects such as PNC Park, Heinz Field and the reconstructed David L. Lawrence Convention Center, could be considered a third Renaissance. That period also could include the growth of Downtown's Cultural District, construction of Three PNC Plaza along Fifth Avenue and plans for Point Park University's Academic Village at Wood Street.

As Pittsburgh's steel industries laid off thousands of workers through the 1980s, the foundation laid by the first post-war period of rebirth helped the region survive, both economically and culturally, though much of the city's early history was wiped clean for redevelopment.

DAVID L. LAWRENCE

David Leo Lawrence was born June 18, 1889, and was Pittsburgh's only four-term mayor, serving from 1946 to 1959.

He once said he learned as a boy to compromise because he and his brothers weren't permitted to fight.

Lawrence was named state chair of the Democratic Party in 1934 and put in place the Democratic machine that is still running today, breaking the decades-long Republican stronghold on city hall during the Great Depression.

That did not prevent him from forging a relationship with financier Richard King Mellon, a Republican. The two shared little in common politically, but they drove Renaissance I, one of the first urban renewal plans in the country and the first serious attempt to stem the city's industry-related pollution.

In 1942, two of Lawrence's sons were killed in a car crash. Perhaps as a result, he spent much of his career promoting and passing some of the toughest highway safety laws in the nation.

After his term as governor from 1959 to 1963, Lawrence was appointed chairman of the President's Committee on Equal Opportunities in Housing in the John F. Kennedy and Lyndon B. Johnson administrations.

He collapsed at a political rally in Pittsburgh on November 4, 1966. He died 17 days later.

RICHARD KING MELLON

Born into the Mellon banking family on June 19, 1899, Richard King Mellon would make a name for himself through not only his business acumen, but his philanthropy and his hand in Pittsburgh's revitalization.

In 1933, after working at various positions in the family business, Mellon took over as president of Mellon Bank. In his 33 years as president and then chairman, the bank underwent rapid growth and helped establish Pittsburgh as a major financial and corporate center.

A veteran of both World Wars, Mellon served in the United States Army Reserve in peacetime, achieving the rank of lieutenant general.

After World War II, he made it his mission to bring Pittsburgh into the modern era with new buildings Downtown and as a center for medicine, research and education. Time magazine lauded his efforts on its cover, calling the revitalization "Mellon's Miracle."

In 1947, he created the Richard King Mellon Foundation, now among the largest independent foundations in the country. With assets totaling more than $2 billion as of 2006, the foundation makes grants primarily in Southwestern Pennsylvania in the areas of economic development, land preservation and watershed restoration and protection.

He died June 3, 1970.

RICHARD S. CALIGUIRI

Mayor Richard S. Caliguiri guided Pittsburgh through the steel industry's death throes to a second Renaissance that included construction of a subway system and the skyscrapers One PPG Place, One Oxford Centre and One Mellon Center.

Elected in 1977, Caliguiri earned a reputation as a quiet, but determined, consensus builder who cared little for fame or politics, but eventually became one of the city's most popular mayors.

A Democrat, he fostered development of Station Square on the South Side and the Pittsburgh Technology Center in South Oakland.

He made inspecting and repairing Pittsburgh's many bridges a priority early in his administration, spent millions of dollars patching potholes and promoted urban renewal in hopes of reversing the city's population decline.

Caliguiri, 56, died on May 7, 1988, of complications from amyloidosis, a potentially fatal build-up of proteins in the organs, during his third term in office.

A statue of the Greenfield native stands in front of the City-County Building, Downtown, and athletes celebrate his life each September in the 10K race he started in 1977 that bears his name.

He is buried in Hazelwood's Calvary Cemetery, as are former Mayors David L. Lawrence and Bob O'Connor.

NOTABLE PHILANTHROPISTS

Charles Avery

Source of wealth: *Cotton mill, mining, bridge building, natural gas*

Charles Avery made a fortune in Pittsburgh but became better known as an abolitionist and financier for causes to benefit the black community before the Civil War.

Born in New York about 1784, Avery moved to Pittsburgh at age 28 to become a druggist and later spread out into other businesses. He helped organize the Methodist Protestant church and incorporate Allegheny Cemetery where he is buried.

He founded the Allegheny Institute and Mission Church, which became Avery College, to educate black students in North America. His estate provided scholarships for them at many colleges, including present-day University of Pittsburgh, Oberlin College and Wilberforce University. He died in 1858.

Michael Benedum

Source of wealth: *Gas and oil*

Michael and Sarah Benedum created the Claude Worthington Benedum Foundation in 1959 and named it for their only child, who died when he was just 20.

With more than $425 million in assets, the foundation targets two-thirds of its giving in West Virginia and the remaining third in Southwestern Pennsylvania.

The foundation seeks to promote education, health and human services, and community and economic development in West Virginia and education and economic development in Southwestern Pennsylvania. The old Stanley Theater became the Benedum Center for the Performing Arts because the foundation awarded the largest grant for the theater's $42 million restoration.

Andrew Carnegie

Source of wealth: *Steel*

At age 66, Andrew Carnegie sold the Carnegie Steel Company, which became United States Steel Company in 1901, to become the richest man in the world. He devoted his life to giving away his fortune.

He built more than 2,000 public libraries around the country, founded what are now the Carnegie Museums of Pittsburgh and Carnegie Mellon University.

Carnegie gave $125 million for the Carnegie Corporation. He set up the Carnegie Endowment for International Peace and built the Hague Palace of Peace, site of the World Court, in the Netherlands.

By 1911 Carnegie had given away $350 million or 90 percent of his wealth. His foundations have given away nearly $2 billion.

Howard Heinz

Vira Heinz

The Heinz Family

Source of wealth: *Food processing*

The foundations of Howard Heinz and of Vira Heinz, his sister-in-law, combined in January 2007 to form The Heinz Endowments, the second-biggest foundation in the region with $1.6 billion in assets.

Heinz is a key player in the life of the city. Its grant-making covers the arts, education, economic development, the environment and youth programs.

The foundation has launched the Pittsburgh Cultural Trust, renovated Loew's Penn Theater into Heinz Hall and has provided funding to the Heinz History Center and the Heinz School of Public Policy and Management at Carnegie Mellon University.

The foundation gives away an average of $60 million a year.

September 8, 2005: Henry and Elsie Hillman during a celebration at the Carnegie Museum of Natural History.

STEVEN ADAMS/TRIBUNE-REVIEW

The Hillmans

Source of wealth: *Venture capital and real estate*

Henry and Elsie Hillman established the Hillman Foundation in 1951 to improve the quality of life in the region.

Their generosity has resulted in the Hillman Hall of Minerals and Gems at the Carnegie Museum of Natural History, the Hillman Cancer Center and the Hillman Library at the University of Pittsburgh.

Other groups supported by the Hillmans include the Pittsburgh Life Sciences Greenhouse, the Children's Museum of Pittsburgh, Allegheny Valley School and the Pittsburgh Parks Conservancy.

The Hillmans also made a major gift to the Waters Edge exhibit at the Pittsburgh Zoo & PPG Aquarium. They reside in Squirrel Hill.

Charles L. McCune

Source of wealth: *Banking*

Charles L. McCune, a Pittsburgh native born on September 24, 1895, was a director of The Union National Bank of Pittsburgh for 56 years, its president from 1945 to 1972 and as chairman until his death on October 16, 1979. A foundation was established in 1979 by his will to enable communities and nonprofit institutions to improve the quality of life. It is one of the largest foundations in Western Pennsylvania and makes contributions as McCune did during his lifetime – as an anonymous donor. He established the foundation in memory of his parents, Janet Walker Lockhart McCune and John Robison McCune.

Thomas Mellon

The Mellon Family

Source of wealth: *Banking, oil and aluminum*

The descendants of Judge Thomas Mellon founded the biggest philanthropic empire in Southwestern Pennsylvania and became one of the most prominent patrons of the arts in America.

Thomas Mellon's son, former United States secretary of the treasury Andrew Mellon, established the National Gallery of Art in Washington, D.C.; Andrew Mellon's son, Paul, also contributed extensively to the National Gallery, along with the Center for British Art, the Virginia Museum of Fine Arts and Yale University.

The Andrew W. Mellon Foundation aids museums, higher education, research in information technology, the performing arts and the environment.

Richard King Mellon, chairman of Mellon Bank, founded the Richard King Mellon Foundation in 1947. The region's largest foundation, with more than $2 billion in assets, it supports conservation, economic development, programs for children and young adults, education and human services.

Sebastian Mueller

Source of wealth: *Food processing*

As vice president and director of the H.J. Heinz Company, Sebastian Mueller and his wife Elizabeth Heinz gave medical care and financial assistance to women long before company health plans and government aid.

In 1938, the year he died, Mueller willed his entire estate, including his summer home in Gibsonia, to help women. Called Eden Hall Farm, it was used as a retreat for Heinz's working and retired female employees and other local women.

His will was broadened in 1983 to create the Eden Hall Foundation, which helps the poor through education, health facilities and other projects. In May, the foundation donated the 338-acre farm to Chatham University. The land is valued at more than $17.5 million.

EVERETT RAYMOND KINSTLER/CARNEGIE MUSEUM OF ART
Portrait of Sarah Mellon Scaife

Henry Phipps

Source of wealth: *Steel and real estate*

Henry Phipps, co-owner of the Carnegie Steel Company, sold his share of the steel firm in 1901 and, like Andrew Carnegie, entered a life of philanthropy. His biggest local contribution: the Phipps Conservatory and Botanical Gardens. Phipps said he wanted to "erect something that will prove a source of instruction as well as pleasure to the people." He further required that it stay open on Sundays so that workers could visit it on their day of rest.

Built in 1893 at a cost of $100,000, the conservatory was made of material from the World's Columbian Exhibition, which closed that year in Chicago. In 1902, Phipps also paid for the addition of the Cacti House.

Like many of Pittsburgh's millionaires, Phipps built a home in New York City. Concerned about the threat of tuberculosis, he built public housing for workers there, including black workers who were the victims of housing discrimination.

The Scaife Family

Source of wealth: *Banking and oil*

In the late 1940s, Sarah Scaife, an heir to the Mellon fortune, equipped a virus research lab at the University of Pittsburgh. It was there that Doctor Jonas Salk found a polio vaccine.

Upon her death in 1965, her son, Tribune-Review owner and publisher Richard M. Scaife, directed the family's charity through the Sarah Scaife, Carthage, Allegheny and the Scaife Family foundations. These foundations support economic development, the arts, education, social programs and drug and alcohol rehabilitation.

The Allegheny Foundation provided all the seed money for the development of Station Square. The Sarah Scaife Foundation and the Scaife family provided funding for construction of the Sarah Scaife Galleries, which house the Carnegie Museum of Art in Oakland.

Other beneficiaries include think tanks and political causes.

Mary Schenley

Source of wealth: *Real estate*

One of Pittsburgh's earliest philanthropists, Mary Schenley shocked two nations. At age 15, Mary Croghan eloped and married Captain Edward W. Schenley, 27 years her senior, and moved to his native England. Their elopement caused her father to faint and get a law passed that protected her fortune.

In 1889, Edward Bigelow, the city's director of public works, sent a lawyer to England to ask Schenley, then a widow, to donate land for a park. She donated 300 acres and gave the city an option to buy 120 acres for a nominal price. That land became Schenley Park.

She also donated land for West Penn Hospital, the Western Pennsylvania Institute for the Blind and the Newsboys' Home; the Fort Pitt Block House and the site of Fort Duquesne; and money for Riverview Park. According to one estimate, she was worth nearly $50 million at the time of her death in 1903.

Henry and Anne Childs Shaffer Phipps

LIBRARY OF CONGRESS

CHAPTER 6

conflict, mayhem AND disasters

"We are being hijacked!"

– A FRIGHTENED MAN TELLS WESTMORELAND COUNTY'S EMERGENCY CENTER DURING A CELL PHONE CALL FROM UNITED AIRLINES FLIGHT 93 ON SEPTEMBER 11, 2001.

Western Pennsylvania was born of war and suffering. History tells of horrific battles for the wilderness.

Pittsburgh was forged by fire and flood. Misery was to be expected with every winter thaw. In the early days when most houses were made of wood, one spark could cause catastrophe, and often did.

Hundreds of historical markers dot the area, telling of the foibles and of the triumphs of the human spirit and of mind-numbing tragedy – hundreds dead in mine disasters or in floods or in industrial accidents; labor disputes that became pitched, deadly battles that stunned the nation.

No matter how wounded or devastated, Pittsburgh bound up its wounds and moved ahead. Some deeds of its sons and daughters will never be forgotten; but others have faded into time.

54

Flood of 1907: People use rowboats on Federal Street in Allegheny City. Floodwaters crested at 38.5 feet on March 15, 1907. The water receded and five days later, crested again at 25.4 feet. Heavy rains had followed a snowfall of 4 to 8 inches across Western Pennsylvania. Electrical storms wiped out telegraph and telephone services, limiting transmission of flood warnings. The area had been hit by a flood in January 1907, and civic leaders petitioned the federal government for flood-control measures. But nothing happened. In 1913, Pittsburgh suffered through four floods.

French and Indian War

On May 28, 1754, Lieutenant Colonel George Washington, dispatched to the Ohio Valley by the royal governor of Virginia, attacked a French reconnaissance party at Jumonville Glen – about 50 miles from Pittsburgh – starting the French and Indian War. The French defeated Washington July 3 at Fort Necessity. More defeats followed for the British. An expedition under General Edward Braddock was annihilated on July 9, 1755, at present-day Braddock. Of 1,400 British soldiers, 900 were casualties. Braddock suffered mortal wounds and died four days later.

Washington had four bullets pass through his coat and two horses shot from under him, but was not wounded.

On September 14, 1758, Major James Grant lost a third of his 800-man force during a skirmish on the site of present-day Grant Street.

The British later took Fort Duquesne without firing a shot; the French burned and evacuated it in advance of General John Forbes' army. The British flag flew over the ruins on November 25, 1758.

On February 10, 1763, the British and French signed the Treaty of Paris, ending the war with the British victorious.

Pontiac's Rebellion

In the early days of the French and Indian War, the British colonial government signed a treaty with the Shawnee, Delaware and other tribes, promising not to settle west of the Allegheny Mountains if the Indians remained neutral. When the war ended and the British didn't leave by May of 1763, a confederation of tribes attacked in Pontiac's Rebellion. That summer, 500 settlers crowded behind the walls of Fort Pitt. In one of the first instances of biological warfare, British officers gave blankets from the smallpox ward to emissaries from the Delaware.

At Bushy Run, about 25 miles from the Point, about 450 English troops under Colonel Henry Bouquet defeated as many as 300 Indians at Bushy Run on August 5 and 6, 1763. As masters of hit-hide-and-run combat, the native tribes tasted defeat for the first time in woodlands fighting. Bouquet was hailed a hero.

The Indians lifted the siege at Fort Pitt in August. Skirmishes would continue for two more years across the frontier, but Fort Pitt never again came under Indian attack.

ROBERT GRIFFING

"On the Trail to Fort Pitt" A band of Mingo warriors pauses on the heights overlooking where the Allegheny and Monongahela rivers merge into the Ohio River. The Mingo, Indians of Iroquois descent who have settled in Western Pennsylvania and the Ohio Country, are on their way to trade furs at Fort Pitt. The fort was not only an important military post, it had become a thriving trade center as well.

Whiskey Rebellion

The new American government passed a tax on distilled spirits in 1791. Smaller producers had to pay at a higher rate, angering Western frontier farmers, who turned most of their surplus grain into alcohol because it was easier to transport to faraway markets. In 1794, federal officials tried to bring tax evaders to court. A mob surrounded Bower Hill, the mansion of tax collector John Neville. Two rebel leaders and an army officer were killed, and the mob burned down the mansion.

Rebels gathered by the thousands at nearby Braddock's Field and marched on Pittsburgh. President George Washington personally led a force of 13,000 federal militia to restore order. Most rebels who were arrested were acquitted for lack of evidence. Washington pardoned the rest, but the Whiskey Rebellion firmly established federal authority over the young nation.

Allegheny Arsenal Explosion

On September 17, 1862, as Union and Confederate troops clashed at Antietam, 78 people died in an explosion at the Allegheny Arsenal in the worst civilian disaster of the Civil War. Black powder from the large munitions works in Lawrenceville escaped from leaky barrels and sifted through floorboards in supply wagons.

A coroner's jury blamed sparks from an iron horseshoe for lighting the powder, which then ignited several barrels of explosives piled on an arsenal porch. This destroyed a building where workers, mostly young girls, assembled cannon shells and rifle cartridges. Today the site of the explosion is a park.

SENATOR JOHN HEINZ HISTORY CENTER

1845: Piers were all that was left of the Monongahela River Bridge after The Great Fire, which destroyed a third of the city.

The Great Fire

Thanks to dry, windy weather and poorly working fire hydrants, a backyard fire to heat water for laundry on April 10, 1845, quickly became a conflagration that consumed 1,100 buildings, including the homes of 700 families. The damage in present-day dollars ranged from $38 million to $68 million. But fewer than five people died, and Pittsburgh was quickly rebuilt.

The 1889 Tornado

Newspapers from as far away as Atlanta reported a tornado striking the city on January 9, 1889, blowing apart a seven-story building under construction near Market Square. The debris demolished or damaged at least six other buildings and buried people alive. Damage from the twister also occurred in the Strip District, Allegheny City, McKeesport and Wilmerding. At least 14 people died and at least 40 people were injured.

SKETCH BY THEODORE R. DAVIS/CARNEGIE LIBRARY OF PITTSBURGH

1874: "The Search for the Dead" Butcher's Run Flood, O'Hara Street.

Butcher's Run Flood

Intense thunderstorms on July 26, 1874, dumped torrents of water. The worst hit was the valley stretching from the North Side to the North Hills around Butcher's Run – a creek named for the many tanneries, glue factories and other livestock businesses.

More than 100 people died in the floods at Butcher's Run and other local creeks, though Pittsburgh and Allegheny City were spared heavy damage. The disaster – and a much worse one at Johnstown 15 years later – led to construction of improved storm drains in the ravines. Many are still in use today.

57

The Johnstown Flood

Residents of Johnstown were caught by surprise May 31, 1889, when a 40-foot wall of water slammed into the city after the South Fork Dam burst 14 miles upstream following days of heavy rains. In all, 2,209 people were killed, including 99 entire families and 396 children. Bodies were found as far away as Cincinnati and as late as 1911. At least 1,600 homes were destroyed and property damage totaled $17 million.

Johnstown has had subsequent major floods, including one in 1936 that killed 24 people and another in 1977 that killed 85.

1889: People survey the damage of the Johnstown Flood. Note the man sitting on the tree that crashed into the house.

Henry Clay Frick's Attempted Assassination

Reading about Henry Clay Frick's role in the 1892 Homestead Strike, the young lovers and radical anarchists Alexander Berkman and Emma Goldman resolved to make an example of him. Breaking into Frick's Downtown office on July 23, 1892, Berkman shot the Carnegie Steel chairman twice in the neck and stabbed his leg repeatedly. Frick survived and was back at work within a week.

Berkman served 14 years in Western Penitentiary. He and Goldman were deported to the Soviet Union in 1919, but soon became disillusioned with the Bolsheviks and left for Germany. Berkman shot himself in 1936.

Mrs. Soffel

Married to the warden of Allegheny County's jail, Kate Soffel fell in love with inmate Edward Biddle, who, with his brother, John, had been sentenced to hang for murder. She helped the brothers escape on January 30, 1902.

Law officers tracked the trio to Butler County and gunned them down. The brothers soon died from their wounds. Soffel, who was injured, spent 19 months in prison and worked the rest of her life as a seamstress, living with her sister. The story was turned into a 1984 film, "Mrs. Soffel," starring Mel Gibson and Diane Keaton.

CARNEGIE LIBRARY OF PITTSBURGH

Crime of Passion

Coke heir Harry Thaw, rumored to have had many sordid affairs with young women, did not settle down to domestic bliss in 1905 when he married Evelyn Nesbit, a Tarentum-born beauty and "Gibson Girl" model. Thaw was incensed that his wife had been the lover of architect Stanford White, when she was 16. On their honeymoon, Thaw used a belt to beat the details out of his bride.

When Thaw spotted White at a rooftop gala and theatrical premiere at Madison Square Garden in New York City on June 25, 1906, he shot his rival in the head. It became the first "Crime of the Century" of the 1900s. Testifying at the trial, Nesbit became famous as "The Girl in the Red Velvet Swing," for a contraption at White's love nest. An insanity defense saved Thaw, but the couple's stormy relationship ended after Nesbit had a child while he was in a mental hospital.

Coal Mine Explosions

On January 25, 1904, 179 men died in the explosion of the Harwick Mine in Allegheny County, believed to have started when a small amount of dust ignited in the mine shaft. Eight men died trying to reach the entombed men, prompting Andrew Carnegie to establish the Carnegie Medal to honor ordinary citizens for extraordinary acts of heroism.

The Darr Mine Disaster on December 19, 1907, killed 239 men and boys – many of them Hungarian immigrants – and helped make that year the deadliest in United States mining history. The disaster in Van Meter, Westmoreland County, ranks as the nation's third worst.

It came days after the December 6 explosion at a mine in Monongah, West Virginia, that killed 358 workers, mostly Italian immigrants. In all, the Mine Safety and Health Administration recorded 3,242 mine deaths in 1907, including 1,400 in Pennsylvania. That year's 18 coal mine disasters spurred Congress to create the United States Bureau of Mines.

HISTORICAL SOCIETY OF WESTERN PENNSYLVANIA

December 19, 1907: Rescue party at Darr Mine Explosion, Jacob's Creek, Pennsylvania.

Aetna Chemical Company Explosion

About 200 residents of South Fayette lost their lives on May 18, 1918, when several explosions destroyed the Aetna Chemical Company's manufacturing plant near Oakdale, which had been making the explosive TNT for the war effort.

The explosions damaged property for miles. A newspaper account from that time lists 96 dead, 59 unaccounted for and 91 injured. A four-sided monument erected by the company at the Oakdale Cemetery reads: "Their lives were devoted to the manufacture of materials necessary to the United States in the prosecution of the war against Germany. Like soldiers they died in their country's service."

Floodwaters inundated the Point, but even in neighborhoods and communities untouched by the water, people were in danger. For days, there was no drinking water, no power and no telephone service. Fires broke out and trapped people in their homes.

The flood left display cases in a jumble on the first floor of the Joseph Horne department store, Downtown.

The Great Saint Patrick's Day Flood 1936

Following a winter that dumped more than 63 inches of snow on Pittsburgh, several inches of rain drenched the region in mid-March, including 1.75 inches on Saint Patrick's Day. River waters rose to 21 feet above flood stage at the Point – so high that people were rescued by rowboat from the second and third floors of buildings. More than 60 people died and 500 were injured.

The subsequent federal Flood Control Act of 1936 has prevented $11 billion in flood damage, according to United States Army Corps of Engineers estimates. It built 16 dams and reservoirs in the region and completed more than 40 flood-control projects.

Thanksgiving Blizzard

For sheer accumulation, nothing beats the Thanksgiving storm of 1950. Starting the day after Thanksgiving, 30.5 inches of snow fell in 60 hours, continuing almost without stop for three days and nights. Municipal road crews were at a loss. If residents wanted their street cleared, they pitched in and did it themselves. At least 50 people in Western Pennsylvania died. Industry virtually shut down. Mail delivery stopped. Damages were estimated at more than $1 million, including lost wages and the cost of plowing. The storm had far-reaching implications beyond the region too – setting record-low temperatures throughout Southeastern states and causing flooding on the eastern side of the Appalachian Mountains.

1950: Vehicles were left in the middle of Webster Avenue in the Hill District as the Thanksgiving storm made roads impassable.

Missing Plane in the Mon

On the morning of January 31, 1956, a B-25 Mitchell mid-range bomber dropped into the Monongahela River downstream from the current Homestead Grays Bridge – instantly becoming part of local lore and national conspiracy theories. The plane had been on its way from Las Vegas to Harrisburg when its crew reported running out of fuel. The plane landed on the water and sunk. Two crew members died.

The plane has never been found, giving rise to conspiracy theories about whether the military secretly pulled it up and carried it away – somehow without the public noticing.

Fatal Crash

Twenty-one people died on April 1, 1956, when an eastbound TWA plane crashed just after takeoff from Greater Pittsburgh Airport. Fourteen people survived. It was the first disaster at the airport since it opened in 1952.

The 1968 Riots

As in cities across the United States, the assassination of Martin Luther King Jr. on April 4, 1968, led to rioting in the streets of Pittsburgh and other major cities. Pittsburgh's riots started the day after King died and continued for a week. One report listed 505 fires across the city, $620,000 in property damage, one death and 926 arrests.

Much of the local unrest focused along Centre Avenue in the Hill District, a first-immigrant neighborhood east of Downtown that had become more concentrated with black residents after World War II. Much of the Lower Hill District had been razed to make space for the Civic Arena, which opened in 1961.

The Yablonski Murders

On New Year's Eve 1969, United Mine Workers of America reformer Joseph "Jock" Yablonski, his wife, Margaret, 57, and their daughter, Charlotte, 25, were murdered in their sleep in the family's stone farm house in East Bethlehem Township. Just three weeks earlier, Yablonski had lost to incumbent Tony Boyle in a bitterly contested campaign for union president.

Yablonski, who had pledged to clean up the organization and end nepotism, had asked the United States Department of Justice to investigate possible election fraud. Boyle and three men he allegedly hired and paid from union accounts – Paul Gilly, Aubran "Buddy" Martin and Claude Vealey – were charged and convicted in the shootings. Boyle got a life sentence and died in prison in 1985.

Gulf Building Explosion

After most people had gone home on the evening of June 13, 1974, a bomb exploded on the 28th floor of the Gulf Building, Downtown, knocking out walls and leaving holes in the floor and ceiling. No one was injured.

The Weather Underground, a radical group from the 1960s, quickly claimed responsibility. In a letter to The Associated Press, it blamed the Gulf Oil Corporation for committing "enormous crimes" by drilling oil in Angola and paying royalties to the Portuguese government, which controlled the colony. Gulf officials called the group "extremists" and said it could do more good for African nationals by staying in Angola rather than leaving.

Three Mile Island Nuclear Accident

At 4 a.m. on the morning of March 28, 1979, a series of malfunctions inside Unit 2 of the Three Mile Island nuclear power generator, 10 miles southeast of Harrisburg, led to a partial meltdown of the reactor's core and small releases of radioactive material into the air.

No one died or suffered significant injuries.

The accident led to major changes in nuclear accident response training and tighter federal regulations while adding to the public's distrust of nuclear power. The partial meltdown remains the nation's worst nuclear accident.

Nick Perry Lottery Scam

When the Pennsylvania Lottery's Daily Number came up 6-6-6 on April 24, 1980, many of the 6 million Pennsylvanians watching on television might have seen an omen. Nick Perry, a Pittsburgh broadcast pioneer, and Edward Plevel, a Pennsylvania Lottery official, had weighted all the balls except those numbered 4 and 6, so only those numbers were light enough to be picked by the machines. Then, with several partners, they bet heavily on combinations of those two numbers.

Within a year, Perry and several others were convicted. Three security officials, a certified public accountant, another accountant and two senior citizen witnesses attend each drawing now to ensure fairness. Pennsylvania's is the only known state lottery-fixing scandal.

PAUL VATHIS/AP IMAGES

May 20, 1981: Nick Perry, center, and Edward Plevel, right, smile as they leave for dinner while a jury in Harrisburg deliberated their fate. The jury later convicted them of fixing the Pennsylvania Lottery. Bookies who paid out illegal bets based on Lottery numbers had suspected a fix and notified authorities after 6-6-6 was drawn on April 24, 1980.

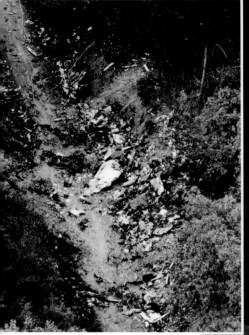

1994: The ruins of USAir Flight 427 in Beaver County.

USAir Flight 427

On its September 8, 1994, approach to Pittsburgh International Airport with 132 people on board, USAir Flight 427 from Chicago suddenly rolled to the left and spiraled to the ground in 28 seconds. There were no survivors.

Initially the crash was blamed on wind patterns because the plane had just passed through the wake turbulence of a plane about 4 miles, or 70 seconds, ahead. But after five years of study, federal investigators with the National Transportation Safety Board determined that a valve in the rudder control unit – about the size of a soup can – had jammed, causing the roll. Federal regulators believe this finding has saved countless lives by preventing similar accidents.

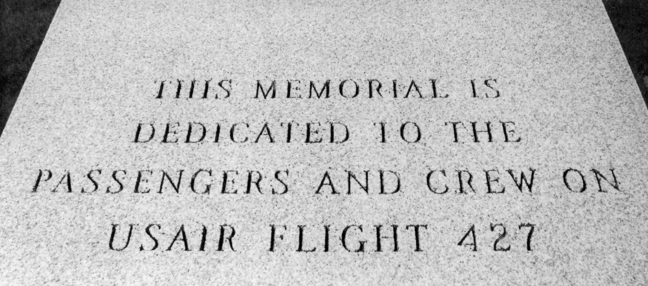

THIS MEMORIAL IS DEDICATED TO THE PASSENGERS AND CREW ON USAIR FLIGHT 427

September 2, 1999: Dawn at the USAir Flight 427 Memorial at Sewickley Cemetery.

Tornadoes

A tornado struck the city around 6 p.m. on June 3, 1998, causing $9 million worth of damage as it tore up 828 buildings, many of them in Mount Washington. Seven buildings in Pittsburgh were destroyed but no one was killed and injuries were minor. Four people were treated in area hospitals, and emergency officials said 20 people had reported injuries.

City officials declared a state of emergency, while the state set one for Allegheny County and 13 other counties. A funnel cloud was spotted in the city about 90 minutes after the twister hit, but it never touched the ground. Tornadoes struck Rankin as well as portions of Beaver and Westmoreland counties. Two people died in Wyoming County in Northeast Pennsylvania.

GUY WATHEN/TRIBUNE-REVIEW

2006: A single mourner is drawn to the crash site of United Airlines Flight 93 near Shanksville just after dawn. Since September 11, 2001, hundreds of thousands of people have paid their respects to the victims.

United Airlines Flight 93

On the morning of September 11, 2001, after planes had slammed into New York City's World Trade Center towers and the Pentagon in Northern Virginia, Pittsburgh officials worried about a fourth plane that had been near Cleveland when it veered off course toward Western Pennsylvania. United Airlines Flight 93 crashed at 10:03 a.m. that day in the tiny community of Shanksville, 80 miles east of Pittsburgh, killing all 40 people on board.

Four hijackers commandeered the San Francisco-bound jetliner that had departed from Newark, New Jersey, directing it toward Washington, D.C. Passengers attempted to take back the plane. The federal 9/11 commission later determined the hijackers crashed the plane to prevent the passengers from regaining control. A permanent National Park Service memorial is scheduled to open on the 10th anniversary of the crash.

GUY WATHEN/TRIBUNE-REVIEW

2002: An exhausted miner is helped out of a rescue capsule after spending 77 hours trapped 239 feet underground.

Quecreek Mine Rescue

Nine miners had been more than a mile from the mine portal when they accidentally breached an abandoned mine, unleashing millions of gallons of bone-chilling water. Nine miners in another section managed to escape. The Quecreek Mine rescue played out on national television over four days, culminating in the early hours of July 28, 2002, with the improbable recovery of all nine trapped miners.

65

October 11, 1910: The Allegheny County Soldiers Memorial in Oakland was dedicated with three days of ceremony, starting with a parade of Civil War veterans on October 10. Speeches and the dedication ceremony took place October 11, and Ladies Day was the day after. The memorial, initially honoring veterans of the Civil War, is now called the Soldiers & Sailors Military Museum and Memorial, and it honors those who served in all military branches in all wars.

soldiering

From settlers' militias formed to protect against Indian attacks on the Allegheny frontier to the rocky terrain of Afghanistan, Pittsburghers have answered the call to defend their country for more than 250 years.

On land, air and sea – or in the mines, mills and factories – they served America.

Citizen soldiers left their farms to fight the French and Indian and Revolutionary wars. During the Civil War, Pittsburghers prepared for a Confederate attack here that never happened while their sons went off to fight at Gettysburg.

In more recent times, exoduses took place from the mills and coal mines to defend liberty during World Wars I and II as well as Korea. Those left behind produced steel, aluminum and coal that built stockpiles of munitions and arms.

Many local young men and women did their duty in Vietnam – as have later generations in Kuwait, Iraq, Afghanistan and other war zones.

Black and white, rich and poor, men and women – the patriotism stood out. Thousands gave their lives and thousands more came home bearing the scars of war. More than 100 Western Pennsylvanians have received the nation's highest military honor – the Medal of Honor.

UNDERGROUND RAILROAD

The Underground Railroad secretly passed slaves from the South to Canada and freedom from the 1830s until the Civil War.

The railroad consisted of clandestine, loosely knit clusters of people, who hid fugitive slaves in barns, attics, cellars, houses and other places.

Southwestern Pennsylvania was a central location for escape routes. It had leaders in the abolition movement and laws in opposition to slavery.

Reputed local stops on the railroad included the Brunot mansion on East Stockton Avenue, in the North Side; the Will T. Fife house in Upper Saint Clair; the Point View Hotel in Brentwood; the Thomas Bingham House on Mount Washington and the Morning Glory Inn, in the South Side.

JACK W. MELTON JR./LIBRARY OF CONGRESS

1864: The Fort Pitt Foundry cast 60 percent of the cannons for the Union army. It cast this 15-inch Rodman Columbiad, called "The Lincoln Gun," that sat at Fort Monroe, Virginia.

FORT PITT FOUNDRY

Close to where the Senator John Heinz History Center sits, The Fort Pitt Foundry and Artillery Proving Grounds cast in 1864 what officers termed a "monster cannon."

Weighing nearly 117,000 pounds and able to hurl a half-ton projectile 5 miles, the United States Army piece remains one of the largest cannons ever forged in this country.

Founded in 1804 by Scotsman Joseph McClurg at what is today Fifth Avenue and Smithfield Street, Downtown, the foundry soon moved to a stretch along the Allegheny River in what is now the Strip District. Guns were tested by firing shot directly into the base of Mount Washington, and later in East Liberty, Shaler and Tarentum. In 1878, the Foundry was bought by a rival, and the remaining ordnance junked or shipped to the Allegheny Arsenal in Lawrenceville.

EMERGENCY OF 1863

From mid-June through early July in 1863, Pittsburgh prepared for invasion by the Confederate Army.

It marked the only time the city was involved militarily in the Civil War.

Tension turned to panic June 11 when a dispatch received by Major General William Brooks, who commanded the United States Army's Department of the Monongahela in Pittsburgh, outlined a probable invasion by Confederate General Robert E. Lee.

Since the beginning of the war, there were worries that Pittsburgh would be a target. Located less than 70 miles from the Mason-Dixon Line, Pittsburgh had a strategic location, heavy manufacturing base, the Fort Pitt Foundry and the Allegheny Arsenal in Lawrenceville.

On Sunday, June 14, city and federal officials decided to close all businesses and factories. Under the supervision of Captain William P. Craighill, with the Corps of Engineers, more than 11,000 men constructed a 12-mile ring of earthen redoubts, powder magazines and batteries.

In all, 37 forts and redoubts were built, finished – ironically – on July 3, the day Lee was defeated at Gettysburg. The Pittsburgh forts were obsolete almost immediately.

Some traces of the fortifications remain in neighborhoods like Northview Heights, Greenfield, Morningside and Herron Hill.

HIGHEST VALOR

At age 19, James Martinus Schoonmaker left what is now the University of Pittsburgh in 1861 to enlist as a private in the Union Army.

By age 20, he was a colonel – believed to be the youngest colonel in the North.

Schoonmaker's actions during the Third Battle of Winchester on September 19, 1864, would earn him the Medal of Honor – one of the first Pittsburghers to receive the nation's highest honor for valor.

Schoonmaker was honored for his actions at Star Fort in the Shenandoah Valley. During a critical period in the battle, he "gallantly led a cavalry charge against the left of the enemy's line of battle, drove the enemy out of his works, and captured many prisoners," according to his citation.

Following his military service, Schoonmaker returned to Pittsburgh and entered the coal mining and coke manufacturing business. He eventually sold his coke interests to the Henry C. Frick Coke Company. He helped found the Pittsburgh & Lake Erie Railroad and became board chairman.

Schoonmaker received his Medal of Honor on May 19, 1899 – 35 years after leading the charge at Fort Star. He died October 11, 1927, at age 85 and is buried in Homewood Cemetery.

Medal of Honor Recipients

CIVIL WAR

Absalom Baird, Army, Washington County
Henry Bingham, Army, Washington County
Hugh Boon, Army, Washington County
Felix Brannigan, Army, Allegheny County
Lewis Brest, Army, Allegheny County
Jeremiah Brown, Army, Armstrong County
Casper Carlisle, Army, Allegheny County
Joseph Chambers, Army, Beaver County
Francis Cunningham, Army, Somerset County
Hiram DeLavie, Army, Allegheny County
John Donaldson, Army, Butler County
James Duncan, Navy, Washington County
Alexander Elliot, Army, Allegheny County
John Ewing, Army, Westmoreland County
Joseph Gion, Army, Allegheny County
Amzi Harmon, Army, Westmoreland County
Francis Herron, Army, Allegheny County
Charles Higby, Army, Beaver County
Thomas Hoffman, Army, Allegheny County
Samuel Johnson, Army, Fayette County
Alexander Kelly, Army, Allegheny County
Thomas Kerr, Army, Allegheny County
John Kindig, Army, Allegheny County
William Leonard, Army, Green County
Cyrus Lower, Army, Lawrence County
Gotlieb Luty, Army, Allegheny County
Milton Matthews, Army, Allegheny County
John Matthews, Army, Westmoreland County
Theodore Mitchell, Army, Allegheny County
Alexander Mitchell, Army, Allegheny County
John Mostoller, Army, Somerset County
Charles Oliver, Army, Westmoreland County
Alfred Pearson, Army, Allegheny County
James Pipes, Army, Greene County
James Purman, Army, Greene County
James Reisinger, Army, Beaver County
Archibald Rowand Jr., Army, Allegheny County
James Schoonmaker, Army, Allegheny County
John Shellenberger, Army, Fayette County
Henry Slusher, Army, Washington County
Michael Sowers, Army, Allegheny County
Jacob Swab, Army, Somerset County
James Thompson, Army, Allegheny County
Andrew Young, Army, Greene County

INDIAN WAR CAMPAIGNS

Albert Glavinski, Army, Allegheny County
Leander Herron, Army, Allegheny County
Michael Himmelsback, Army, Allegheny County
James Huff, Army, Washington County
Henry Mechlin, Army, Allegheny County
Peter Thompson, Army, Allegheny County
Jacob Trautman, Army, Allegheny County
Henry Wilkens, Army, Allegheny County

SPANISH-AMERICAN WAR

Ulysses Buzzard, Army, Allegheny County

PHILIPPINE INSURRECTION

Louis Gedeon, Army, Allegheny County

MEXICAN CAMPAIGN

Charles Bishop, Navy, Allegheny County
Robert Semple, Navy, Allegheny County

BOXER REBELLION

Harry Fisher, Marine Corps, Allegheny County

HAITIAN CAMPAIGN

Ross Iams, Marine Corps, Greene County

WORLD WAR I

James Mestrovitch, Army, Allegheny County
Joseph Henry Thompson, Army, Beaver County

WORLD WAR II

Alvin Carey, Army, Westmoreland County
Leonard Funk Jr., Army, Allegheny County
Charles Kelly, Army, Allegheny County
Donald Lobaugh, Army, Armstrong County
Archibald Mathies, Army Air Corps, Allegheny County
John Minick, Army, Allegheny County
Mitchell Paige, Marine Corps, Washington County
John Pinder Jr., Army, Washington County
William Shomo, Army Air Corps, Westmoreland County
Alfred Wilson, Army, Fayette County

BETWEEN THE WORLD WARS 1920-1940

Henry Drexler, Navy, Allegheny County

KOREAN WAR

John Kelly, Marine Corps, Allegheny County
Frederick Mausert III, Marine Corps, Washington County
George Ramer, Marine Corps Reserves, Somerset County
Clifton Speicher, Army, Somerset County

VIETNAM WAR

Ralph Dias, Marine Corps, Allegheny County
Walter Marm Jr., Army, Allegheny County
William Morgan, Marine Corps, Allegheny County
William Prom, Marine Corps, Allegheny County

WAR IN IRAQ

Ross McGinnis, Army, Clarion County

These Medal of Honor recipients were born in Pennsylvania but had their medals accredited to other states. The list includes the soldier's place of birth as well as the state that is credited for his Medal of Honor:

CIVIL WAR

Thomas Anderson, Army, Scenery Hill, Washington County; West Virginia
Henry Casey, Army, Fayette County; Ohio
William Carson, Army, Washington County; Ohio
James Cunningham, Army, Washington County; Illinois
James Merrifield, Army, Hyde Park, Westmoreland County; Illinois
James Peirsol, Army, Beaver County; Ohio
Reuben Smalley, Army, Washington County; Illinois
Charles Swan, Army, Greene County; Iowa
Joseph Wortick, Army, Fayette County; Missouri

INDIAN WAR CAMPAIGNS

James Hill, Army, Washington Count;, Ohio
John Kirkwood, Army, Allegheny City, Allegheny County; Nebraska
Benjamin Wilson, Army, Pittsburgh, Allegheny County; Ohio

SPANISH-AMERICAN WAR

Robert Blume, Navy, Pittsburgh; New Jersey

WORLD WAR I

George McMurtry, Army, Pittsburgh, Allegheny County; New York

WORLD WAR II

Walter Will, Army, Pittsburgh, Allegheny County; New York

KOREAN WAR

Reginald Desiderio, Army, Clairton, Allegheny County; California
Donn Porter, Army, Sewickley, Allegheny County; Maryland
Raymond Harvey, Army, Ford City, Armstrong County; California

VIETNAM WAR

Michael Estocin, Navy, Turtle Creek, Allegheny County; Ohio
James Graham, Marine Corps, Wilkinsburg, Allegheny County; Maryland
Michael Novosel, Army, Etna, Allegheny County; Louisiana

HAYS

The Allegheny Arsenal, which operated in Lawrenceville from 1814 to 1926, was perhaps the most famous, but it wasn't Pittsburgh's only wartime ammunition plant.

The United States Navy in 1942 built an ammunition manufacturing center in Hays to produce 16-inch howitzer shells used during World War II. It remained open through the Korean and Vietnam conflicts and employed more than 1,000 people.

The United States Army took over the plant in 1966, and shell manufacturing entered its most active period, producing more than 3.8 million projectile casings between 1967 and 1970.

The Army mothballed the 200,000-square-foot plant in 1971, and it was officially decommissioned 17 years later. The Army sold the 12-acre site to the Urban Redevelopment Authority of Pittsburgh for $1 in 1993.

In 1991, actor-director Danny DeVito scouted the Mifflin Road warehouse as a possible soundstage for the movie "Hoffa." That later sparked the URA's idea of converting the space for movie productions. No private developer was found to undertake the project. The warehouse was converted to a steel-plating facility in 1996 and remains open today.

COURTESY OF MARTHA J. WILKINS

The Tuskegee Airmen, like Lieutenant William A. Johnston Jr. of Sewickley, broke the color barrier in the skies during World War II. Nearly 1,000 Tuskegee Airmen were commissioned as pilots by the United States Army Air Corps.

TUSKEGEE AIRMEN

More than 50 men from Southwestern Pennsylvania served as Tuskegee Airmen, the first black military airmen in the United States. Five of them died when they were shot down during combat.

The Tuskegee Airmen came from the Hill District, North Side and Homewood-Brushton. Eight were from Sewickley. Others came from Mars, Yukon, McKeesport, Glassport and Washington.

Breaking the military's racial barrier was difficult. They endured segregation and discrimination and were kept from all-white officers' clubs. In 1948, President Harry Truman ended segregation in all United States armed forces.

Black aviators have a long history in Pittsburgh. Charles Wesley Peters first flew a glider in the Hill District in 1906.

Peters later strapped an automobile engine to a homemade plane and flew 10 trips over Pittsburgh. He flew a second plane he built in 1911 at the Georgia Negro State Fair in Macon.

1918: Veterans march down Fifth Avenue after returning home from World War I.

MEN OF WAR

Charles "Commando" Kelly

Kelly served in the Army during World War II and was the first enlisted man in the European Theater to receive the Congressional Medal of Honor for his actions September 13 and 14, 1943, near Altavilla, Italy.

Kelly volunteered for several hazardous assignments to obtain information about an enemy position. The next day, he was protecting an ammunition storehouse under heavy attack; when a second automatic rifle locked up after becoming overheated, Kelly used 60mm mortar shells as hand grenades until members of his unit could withdraw to safety.

Kelly, a North Side native, was born September 23, 1920, and resided there until his death on January 11, 1985.

Edwin Stanton

Born December 19, 1814, in Steubenville, Ohio, Stanton came to Pittsburgh in 1847 to practice law. He moved to Washington, D.C., in 1856. He served as attorney general under President James Buchanan. Appointed secretary of war in 1862 by President Abraham Lincoln, he held the position under President Andrew Johnson until 1868. President Ulysses S. Grant appointed him to the United States Supreme Court in 1869, but Stanton died on December 24, four days after being confirmed by the Senate.

Stanton is credited with the first use of an insanity defense in the United States, leading to the acquittal of a man charged with murdering his wife's lover in 1859.

General Alexander Hays

As commander of the Union Army's Third Division, Second Corps, Hays broke the final charge of Confederate General George Pickett's men at Gettysburg on July 3, 1863.

Hays, who was born July 8, 1819, in Franklin, also served as a civil engineer for the City of Pittsburgh from 1854 to 1860. He died on May 5, 1864, during the Battle of the Wilderness in Virginia.

George C. Marshall Jr.

Marshall was a World War II general who served as chief military adviser to President Franklin D. Roosevelt. He was born in Uniontown on December 31, 1880. In 1947, he became secretary of state in the administration of President Harry Truman. Marshall outlined the United States' plan to rebuild Europe after the war and it became known as the Marshall Plan. Marshall received the Nobel Peace Prize in 1953. He died October 16, 1959.

General Matthew B. Ridgway

Ridgway was the first commander of the Army's 82nd Airborne Division and planned the Army's first major airborne assault, in Sicily, during World War II. He also led the airborne invasion into Normandy prior to the amphibious landings on June 6, 1944.

In April 1951, Ridgway succeeded General Douglas MacArthur as commander of United Nations forces in the Far East. The next year, he became supreme commander of Allied Forces in Europe. Ridgway was known for his habit of attaching a hand grenade to one shoulder strap on his battle jacket, and a first aid kit on the other. After retiring from the Army in 1955, Ridgway moved to Fox Chapel, where he lived until his death on July 26, 1993, at age 98. He was born March 3, 1895, in Fort Monroe, Virginia.

Michael V. Hayden

Hayden was named director of the Central Intelligence Agency on May 30, 2006. He previously served as the director of the National Security Agency and chief of the Central Security Service. Hayden retired from the United States Air Force in July 2008 with the rank of general.

Hayden has held senior staff positions at the Pentagon, the National Security Council, and the United States Embassy in Sofia, Bulgaria, as well as serving as deputy chief of staff for United Nations Command and United States forces in Korea. Born March 17, 1945, Hayden is a North Side native and graduate of Duquesne University.

June 21, 2006: Since the attacks of September 11, 2001, hundreds of men and women from Western Pennsylvania have served in Iraq and Afghanistan. Private William Russell of Troy Hill gets a welcome-home hug from his sister Ginny Willen upon his return from an 18-month deployment.

November 19, 2007: Two soldiers stand guard over the casket of a fallen colleague. More than 200 soldiers from Pennsylvania have died in Afghanistan and Iraq.

June 6, 2006: The Pennsylvania Air National Guard's 171st Air Refueling Wing in Findlay has helped support military efforts after the 9/11 attacks and in Iraq and Afghanistan. Major Verne Brosky of Hopewell waves an American flag as Lieutenant Colonel Sean Boyle taxies the plane.

CHAPTER 8

technology, medicine AND education

"Mr. Televox" wasn't much to look at – basically an electronic relay switcher and record player mounted inside a cardboard cutout of a robot.

But many call him the world's first working model of a robot, built in the 1920s by Westinghouse Electric Corporation.

Robotics is a key component of the city's economic rebirth – as are computer science, artificial intelligence and life sciences.

More than 7,000 technology firms in the region employ more than 207,000 people and account for 17.5 percent of the area's overall workforce. Their annual payroll is $10.8 billion.

The Pittsburgh Supercomputing Center – a joint effort of University of Pittsburgh, Carnegie Mellon University and Westinghouse – provides high-performance computing systems for research.

A computer program called Logic Theorist, cemented Carnegie Mellon – at the time called Carnegie Institute of Technology – in the top tier of computer science and engineering institutions. Designed by Professor Herbert Simon and student Alan Newell and introduced in 1956, Logic Theorist proved several complicated mathematical theorems and was the first working example of artificial intelligence.

It made the careers of Simon and Newell. Simon later won the Nobel Prize.

A year after Logic Theorist's debut, Pittsburgh again made national high-tech headlines with the opening of an atomic power plant in Shippingport, 25 miles down the Ohio River from the Point.

Initially the reactor was meant to power an aircraft carrier. That project was scrapped, so Westinghouse redesigned the reactor to supply electricity to Duquesne Light's grid. From its groundbreaking in 1954, the Shippingport Atomic Power Station became the centerpiece of President Dwight D. Eisenhower's "Atoms for Peace" plan, and was touted as the world's first nuclear reactor built entirely for peaceful means.

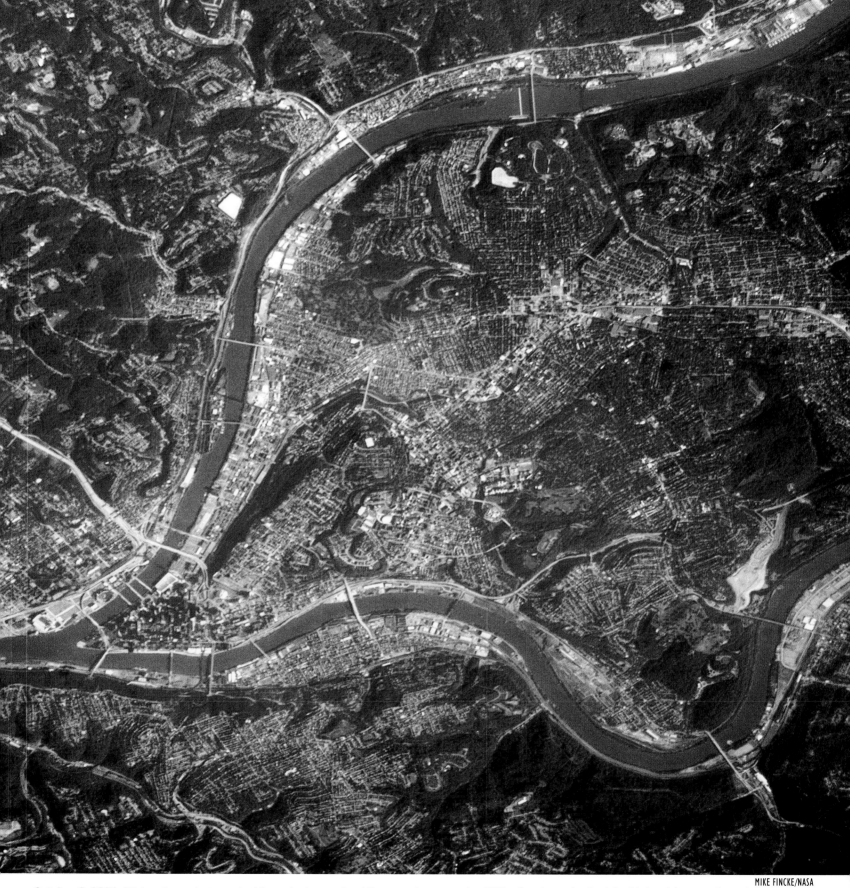

October 8, 2004: Pittsburgh, as photographed from the International Space station more than 200 miles above the Earth by National Aeronautics and Space Administration astronaut Colonel Mike Fincke, an Emsworth native.

75

MEDICINE

Medicine is Western Pennsylvania's new steel. Life-sciences research – propelled by the University of Pittsburgh and Carnegie Mellon University – employs more than 117,000 people in 13 counties with a payroll of nearly $6 billion.

Ever since Doctor Jonas Salk created the polio vaccine at the University of Pittsburgh in 1955, the region has been a magnet for the most accomplished physicians and scientists from around the world.

Pittsburgh has transformed itself into a mecca for medical breakthroughs and scientific milestones. There have been bold initiatives such as trying to cure type 1 diabetes, regenerating limbs and weaning organ transplant patients off harmful anti-rejection drugs.

The region's largest employers are massive hospital networks, such as the University of Pittsburgh Medical Center, a $7 billion enterprise whose 20 hospitals include one in Palermo, Sicily.

Its rival, West Penn Allegheny, is home to the National Surgical Adjuvant Breast and Bowel Project, whose researchers at more than 200 centers have been responsible for changing the standard way to treat some forms of breast cancer.

Pittsburgh ranks among the country's top cities receiving research grants from the National Institutes of Health, the world's largest source of biomedical research.

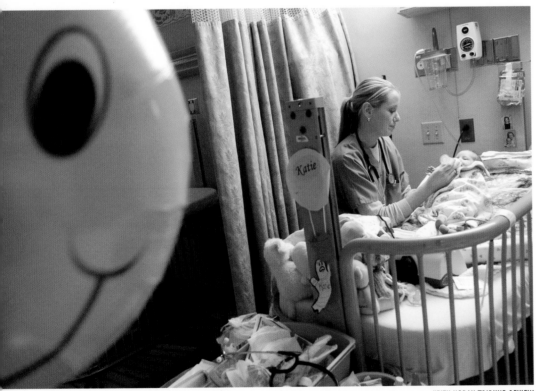

KEITH HODAN/TRIBUNE-REVIEW

Children's Hospital is one of the leading pediatric hospitals in the nation. It will move from Oakland to a new building on the grounds of the old Saint Francis Hospital, Lawrenceville, in 2009.

HEART

Magovern

Pittsburgh heart surgeon George Magovern Sr. changed the face of cardiac medicine at Allegheny General Hospital in the early 1960s.

Magovern, along with engineer Harry Cromie, perfected a sutureless heart valve that clamped into place and reduced surgery time. The titanium device became an industry staple and is credited with saving hundreds of lives.

Magovern, who performed Pennsylvania's first heart valve replacement surgery, later created what became the nation's leading company for heart valve design, Surgitool Corporation. He also was one of the founders of Respironics, the medical device manufacturer in Murrysville.

EMERGENCY MEDICINE

What began in the mid-1960s to give unemployed black men of the Hill District jobs driving huckster wagons evolved into a minority-run ambulance service that was in the vanguard of the civil rights movement and modern emergency medicine.

The Freedom House Enterprises Ambulance Service brought skilled care to the scene, on ambulances equipped like compact intensive-care units.

Until then, such care began at the emergency-room door. Most ambulances were little more than taxis. Many Pittsburghers who needed emergency medical care waited for a police wagon to cart them to a hospital.

Freedom House was a nonprofit community development corporation. Philip Hallen, who was then president of the Maurice Falk Medical Fund, heard about a program to train unemployed black men to drive produce trucks. He approached Freedom House founder and civil rights activist Jim McCoy and suggested the plan be changed to address health-care needs.

Doctor Peter Safar, a University of Pittsburgh Medical School anesthesiologist, had developed a method of cardiopulmonary resuscitation. Freedom House vehicles were designed to his specifications and outfitted with electrocardiogram monitors, intravenous drips, intubation kits, blood pressure cuffs and defibrillators. A curriculum was developed to train emergency medical technicians.

Some consider Freedom House the foundation of emergency medical services in the United States. In 1975, it was absorbed by the city's Emergency Medical Services division.

CARNEGIE LIBRARY OF PITTSBURGH

c. 1895: West Penn Hospital ambulances at the ready.

LIBRARY AND ARCHIVES DIVISION, SENATOR JOHN HEINZ HISTORY CENTER

Freedom House technicians received about 300 hours of classroom and clinical work, followed by nine months of physician-supervised, on-the-job training.

POLIO

Polio was an unstoppable disease. Nearly 58,000 Americans contracted it during the last major epidemic in the United States in 1952. The virus caused paralysis, breathing problems and in many cases death.

The illness has been virtually wiped out thanks to Doctor Jonas Salk, a University of Pittsburgh scientist who developed the first effective polio vaccine assisted by his core research team, which included Army Major Byron L. Bennett, Doctor Percival L. Bazeley, L. James Lewis, Julius S. Youngner, Elsie N. Ward and Francis Yurochko.

The Salk vaccine was made with a dead polio virus, instead of a live virus, to prevent the injections from infecting patients. Hundreds of local schoolchildren tested the vaccine and became known as "polio pioneers."

The vaccine, announced publicly on April 12, 1955, was welcomed by parents as a miracle and cemented Pitt's reputation as a medical research center.

CARNEGIE LIBRARY OF PITTSBURGH

Doctor Jonas Salk and his staff of researchers discovered the cure for polio at the University of Pittsburgh.

JUSTIN MERRIMAN/TRIBUNE-REVIEW

December 16, 2005: The polio virus isolated from Jim Sarkett's blood was used by Doctor Jonas Salk to create the vaccine for polio, saving millions of lives.

TRANSPLANT MEDICINE

In the 1980s, Pittsburgh was known as the organ transplant capital of the world.

Patients from all over the world flocked to the University of Pittsburgh Medical Center, home to the "father of transplantation," Doctor Thomas E. Starzl.

Starzl defined the field in 1967 when he performed the first successful liver transplant at the University of Colorado.

When he joined the University of Pittsburgh School of Medicine and performed the region's first liver transplant in 1981, Starzl transformed a complicated surgery into an everyday procedure. He was chief of organ transplants at Presbyterian University Hospital, now UPMC Presbyterian, until 1991. Starzl also identified better ways to control organ rejection and wean patients off harmful anti-rejection drugs.

Today, more than 11,000 transplants have been performed at UPMC, and two other transplant programs are flourishing, at Allegheny General Hospital in the North Side and the Pittsburgh VA Healthcare System.

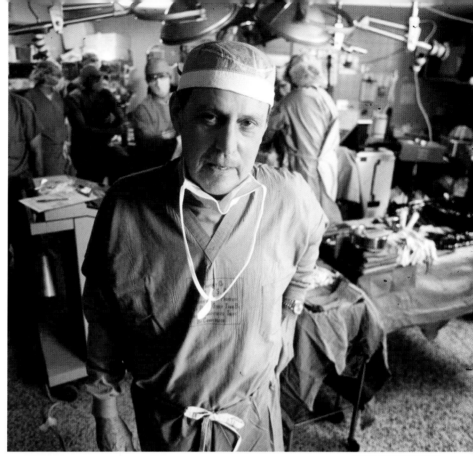

GENE J. PUSKAR/AP IMAGES

November 10, 1989: Pioneer Doctor Thomas E. Starzl helped make Pittsburgh an international center for organ transplants.

February 8, 2004: Pittsburgh is home to two renowned burn centers. Each year burn victims gather at what is now UPMC Mercy on "Burn Survivor Sunday" to celebrate their recoveries.

PHILIP G. PAVELY/TRIBUNE-REVIEW

BURN CENTERS

There are two highly sophisticated burn treatment centers in Western Pennsylvania. The first, at what is now UPMC Mercy, opened in 1967 at the hospital's Uptown campus. The center, established by Doctor Charles E. Copeland, operates under the same roof as the region's only center that can treat the highest level of trauma cases. A 9,000-square-foot, nine-bed unit is dedicated to trauma and burn care.

The area's other burn center opened in 1969, at West Penn Hospital in Bloomfield. It is the only burn center in the tri-state area to be verified by the American Burn Association and American College of Surgeons.

HOSPITALS

The earliest hospital was a military hospital. Hand Hospital opened in 1778 in what is now Crafton. It was named for Brigadier General Edward Hand, the commander of Fort Pitt. It was the first federal hospital in America and a forerunner of the system operated by the United States Department of Veterans Affairs.

Temporary hospitals for the public opened in 1833 for victims of a cholera epidemic and in 1845-46 for victims of a smallpox epidemic. Poor sanitation and living conditions contributed to frequent outbreaks of contagious disease. Industrial accidents were many and required skilled treatment. Permanent hospitals became a necessity. These were the earliest:

Mercy Hospital

Seven Sisters of Mercy opened the first permanent hospital in Pittsburgh on January 1, 1847. For the first 16 months, it was located in a concert hall Downtown. Then it moved to a new building on Stevenson Street at its present location. During the Civil War, the government paid Mercy Hospital 94-cents a day to treat soldiers. Mercy was the region's first teaching hospital with resident physicians in training beginning in 1848. It became part of the University of Pittsburgh Medical Center on January 1, 2008.

Western Pennsylvania Hospital

The Western Pennsylvania Hospital was incorporated in 1848 as Pittsburgh's first public hospital. It was located in the Strip District and opened to patients in 1853. It treated thousands of wounded soldiers during the Civil War and for decades afterward. West Penn moved to Bloomfield in 1912. It has two campuses – The Western Pennsylvania Hospital in Pittsburgh and The Western Pennsylvania Hospital-Forbes Regional Campus in Monroeville.

Dixmont hospital for the mentally ill was part of West Penn when it opened in Kilbuck in 1862. The two hospitals became separate entities in 1907. Dixmont closed in 1984 and was demolished in 2005.

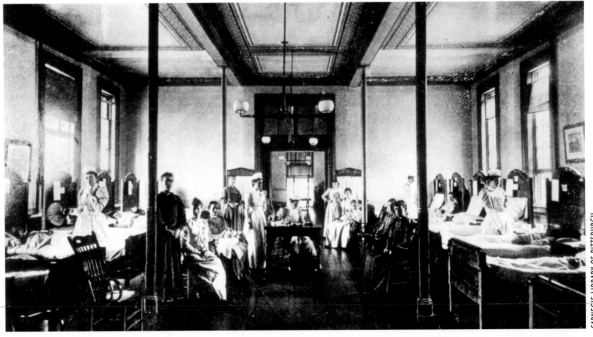

Passavant Hospital

The Reverend W.A. Passavant, assisted by Protestant nuns, opened the Pittsburgh Infirmary in a rented house on Fleming Street in Allegheny City in 1849. Neighbors objected to its location and threatened to burn it down. The infirmary moved to Reed and Roberts streets in the Hill District and opened in 1851, becoming Passavant Hospital, the oldest Protestant hospital in the city. It later moved to McCandless and became part of UPMC in 1997.

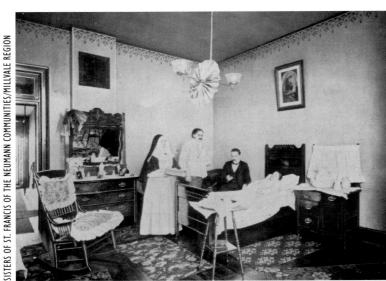

Saint Francis

Sisters of Saint Francis from Buffalo traveled to Pittsburgh in 1865 to solicit donations and were convinced to stay and establish a hospital. The hospital established in Lawrenceville became a flagship for a health system with hospitals in Uptown, Cranberry and New Castle. The Saint Francis Health System closed in 2002. The University of Pittsburgh Medical Center acquired the Lawrenceville campus for the new Children's Hospital of Pittsburgh of UPMC, which is slated to open in 2009.

Shadyside Hospital

The hospital got its start Downtown in 1866 on Second Avenue near Smithfield Street as the Homeopathic Medical and Surgical Hospital and Dispensary. On February 22, 1910, a 160-bed hospital opened in what was then suburban Shadyside. A typical nurse's shift of the day was 12 hours. The Downtown hospital closed in 1915. Shadyside Hospital became part of the UPMC system in 1997 and is the home of the Hillman Cancer Center.

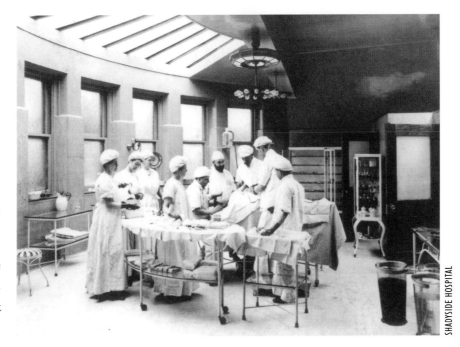

Did you know?

■ In 1851, the federal government opened a hospital for rivermen in Woods Run. The United States Marine Hospital became a clinic in 1949. The federal government closed all marine hospitals and clinics by 1981.

■ After the Battle of Shiloh, April 6-7, 1862, "floating hospitals" were dispatched from Pittsburgh to bring back wounded soldiers.

■ Allegheny General Hospital opened in 1885 on East Stockton Avenue in Allegheny City with a capacity of 100 beds. It moved to its present location on East North Avenue in 1936 with the construction of a 20-story hospital.

■ Pittsburgh Hospital for Children got its start when the young son of a physician raised money to endow a single cot at a local hospital for use only by infants and children. By 1890, enough money had been raised to build a 15-bed hospital in Oakland.

■ Two of Pittsburgh's hospitals were chartered by groups of women: Presbyterian Hospital and Eye and Ear Hospital, both in 1895.

■ Jewish community groups, led by Annie Jacobs Davis, opened Montefiore Hospital in 1908 in a converted building in the Hill District. The hospital gave the growing Jewish population access to care and enabled Jewish doctors to practice medicine without ethnic or religious barriers. In 1929, the hospital moved to Oakland. It became part of the UPMC system at the end of the 1980s.

OLD SCHOOL
These colleges and universities got their start more than a century ago.

University of Pittsburgh

Established as the Pittsburgh Academy in 1786. It became the Western University of Pennsylvania in 1819 and the University of Pittsburgh on July 11, 1908. The Oakland campus is the site of the 42-story Cathedral of Learning, the tallest academic building in the Western Hemisphere. There are 16 schools and colleges in the university, including schools of dentistry, law and medicine.

Some of Pitt's most noted contributions have been in medicine. Charles Glen King and his colleagues isolated vitamin C after five years of research, defeating scurvy. Pitt researchers led by Doctor Jonas Salk discovered the cure for polio. Surgeons Thomas E. Starzl and Henry Bahnson performed the world's first double transplant operation.

The school has an enrollment of 27,000 at the main campus and almost 34,000 attending regional campuses in Bradford, Greensburg, Johnstown and Titusville.

Famous graduates: actor-dancer Gene Kelly; writer Michael Chabon; quarterback Dan Marino; Heisman Trophy winner Tony Dorsett and Olympic gold medal winner John Woodruff.

Washington & Jefferson College

Traces its roots to a cabin school, founded in 1781 in Washington, Pennsylvania, It became Washington Academy and in 1806, Washington College, offering a curriculum of Latin and Greek, arithmetic, chemistry, logic and English grammar. Jefferson College, in Canonsburg, was chartered in 1802 and graduated four students that year with bachelor of arts degrees. The schools merged in 1865 and four years later, all classes moved to Washington. Current enrollment is just over 1,500. The school offers 30 major and 25 minor programs.

Famous graduates: Pittsburgh Mayor Luke Ravenstahl; NFL Commissioner Roger Goodell; 19th-century songwriter Stephen Foster attended, but was expelled.

STEVEN ADAMS/TRIBUNE-REVIEW

2002: Washington & Jefferson College traces its roots to 1781, making it the oldest institution of higher learning in Western Pennsylvania.

SEAN STIPP/TRIBUNE-REVIEW

2006: Saint Vincent College was founded by Benedictine monks on the outskirts of Latrobe.

Saint Vincent College

Founded in 1846 with 18 students. It offered training for the priesthood and a liberal arts program.

The school now has about 1,900 graduate and undergraduate students and offers about 70 major and minor programs at the graduate and undergraduate level.

Famous graduates: Doctor Herbert Boyer, the founder of Genentech Organization, based in San Francisco, and the inventor of gene-splicing technology; William H. Isler, president of Family Communications, Incorporated, which produced "Mr. Rogers' Neighborhood," and president of the board of Pittsburgh Public Schools.

Chatham University

Established in 1870 as the Pennsylvania Female College. It had 103 students enrolled in a general liberal studies curriculum studying language, natural sciences, philosophy, history and the arts. It became Pennsylvania College for Women in 1890 and Chatham College in 1955. It became Chatham University in 2007 with three colleges, one of which, Chatham College for Women, awards degrees to women only. Today there are 1,900 undergraduate and graduate students. The school offers 60 programs of study.

Famous graduates: environmentalist Rachel Carson; state Supreme Court Justice Debra Todd.

2008: Duquesne University was founded in a building on Wylie Avenue. It expanded to its current campus on the Bluff overlooking Forbes Avenue in 1885.

Duquesne University

Founded in 1878 by the Holy Ghost Fathers with 40 students, Duquesne's enrollment stands at more than 10,000. The original offerings included a classical course, a commercial course, a preparatory course and a school for younger boys – all in the School of Liberal Arts.

The school now offers 100 undergraduate degree programs, 66 graduate degree programs and 22 doctorate degree programs offered across 10 schools of study plus degrees in pharmacy and law.

Famous graduates: Central Intelligence Agency Director Michael V. Hayden; musician Bobby Vinton; retired race car driver Chip Ganassi; Steelers President Art Rooney II and Steelers Chairman Dan Rooney.

2008: Carnegie Mellon is one of the preeminent schools for robotics in the world.

Carnegie Mellon University

Founded by Andrew Carnegie in 1900 as Carnegie Technical Schools, the first class enrolled in 1905 studying in the School of Science and Technology, the School of Fine and Applied Arts, the School for Apprentices and Journeymen and the Margaret Morrison Carnegie School for Women. The first class graduated in 1908 with 58 of its original 120 members.

The school became Carnegie Institute of Technology in 1912 and Carnegie Mellon University in 1967 with the merger of Mellon Institute. The school for women was phased out in 1973.

CMU has seven schools and colleges; it enrolls more than 5,700 undergraduate students and nearly 5,000 graduate students. It is a leading research university for computer science and artificial intelligence. The Royal Swedish Academy of Sciences has awarded Nobel Prizes to 15 Carnegie Mellon alumni, faculty and former faculty members and research associates. The College of Fine Arts has produced Academy, Emmy and Tony award winners.

Famous graduates: artist Andy Warhol; actors Ted Danson and Holly Hunter; producer Stephen Bochco; mathematician John Nash, Jr.; director and choreographer Rob Marshall and the late astronaut Judith Resnick.

OTHER ALLEGHENY COUNTY COLLEGES AND UNIVERSITIES

Robert Morris University
founded in 1921

Carlow University
opened in 1929 as Mount Mercy College

Point Park University
founded in 1960

LaRoche College
founded in 1963

Community College of Allegheny
opened in 1966

1947: Smoke and soot rise from the Jones & Laughlin Steel Corporation steel mills on the Monongahela River, as seen from Boulevard of the Allies. Instrumental in improving the city's air quality were the Group Against Smog and Pollution and Michelle Madoff, its founder and first president. GASP was founded in 1969.

GOING GREEN

Pittsburgh's smoke might be as legendary as its steel.

It has been difficult to shake the "Smoky City" label, no matter how many times one might see the panoramic, clear-sky view of Downtown after emerging from the Fort Pitt Tunnel.

Smoke-control ordinances date to 1895 in Pittsburgh. But it wasn't until 1949, after the industrial boom of World War II, that Allegheny County enacted the first smoke-control ordinance, spurred in part by the four-day smog in October 1948 over Donora in Washington County that killed 20 people and sickened 600.

In the 1920s, when area mills were churning, 165.8 tons of dust fell each month per square mile in Allegheny County. In 2006, dust fall per square mile was 20.6 tons per month.

Problem areas remain in Liberty and Clairton, the location of United States Steel Corporation's Clairton Coke Works, the largest coke-making plant in the United States. Reducing fine-particle pollution, specks of soot about 1/30th the width of a human hair, which can aggravate lung and heart problems, is a challenge. A major source of fine-particle pollution is the burning of fossil fuels.

Area waterways are mending after years of abuse. Controls on emissions of industrial waste and sewage have led to a return of long-gone species of fish, insects and wildlife to area streams and rivers.

In 2001, Pittsburgh had its first hatch of mayflies in about 150 years. Fresh water mussels started to return to local waters in the 1980s; now there are at least a half-dozen species.

DAVID L. LAWRENCE CONVENTION CENTER

Pittsburgh became home to an environmental first when the David L. Lawrence Convention Center opened in 2003.

The 1.5-million-square-foot convention center built along the Allegheny River became the largest building to meet rigorous requirements created by the United States Green Building Council for GOLD Leadership in Energy and Environmental Design – and it spurred other "green" construction in the city, making it a national leader.

The $370 million, four-story building has a reclamation system that reduces water use by 50 percent; natural ventilation lessens energy requirements; and recycling bins are placed throughout the building. Almost 75 percent of the exhibition space is lit by daylight.

Before the first beam was set, the project was environmentally conscious. More than 95 percent of demolition waste from the former convention center was recycled.

Pittsburgh has at least 22 other "green" buildings built to standards of the United States Building Council, including the Senator John Heinz History Center in the Strip District.

Green roofs have been installed at Carnegie Mellon University, the University of Pittsburgh, the Children's Museum of Pittsburgh, the Heinz History Center, Phipps Conservatory and Botanical Gardens and the Shadyside Giant Eagle. The roofs contain a four-inch layer of vegetation that helps capture and recycle at least 5,000 gallons of runoff water each year, and reduces energy bills and building emissions.

AIMEE OBIDZINSKI/TRIBUNE-REVIEW

April 20, 2008: The sweeping roof of the David L. Lawrence Convention Center is a dramatic addition to the city's skyline along the Allegheny River.

November 4, 2005: Dawn's early light shimmers on the rivers with the Golden Triangle in silhouette.

CHAPTER 9

KEITH HODAN/TRIBUNE-REVIEW

arts AND architecture

Call it extraordinary – that so many world-renowned musicians, playwrights, writers, artists and actors come from Western Pennsylvania.

Few regions come close.

Big Steel bred Big Money, which bred culture and taste. It helped that Pittsburgh was midway between Chicago and New York. In the days before air travel, big-name talent on tour would always stop in Pittsburgh, sprinkling stardust and dreams.

The city's symphony, ballet and museums are world class. Its architecture is distinctive. Its tradition in theater dates to Colonial days, when British officers staged their own productions of Shakespeare. Today, it is nurtured by Carnegie Mellon University, the University of Pittsburgh, the Civic Light Opera Academy and Point Park University.

So forget about shuffling off to Buffalo.

Pittsburgh is an arts town, and one of the nation's best.

MUSEUMS

The very first museum and fine art gallery in Pittsburgh was founded in 1828 by James Reid Lambdin.

Born in Pittsburgh on May 10, 1807, Lambdin became a portrait painter of considerable note after studying under the distinguished portrait painter Thomas Sully in Philadelphia while a teenager. Lambdin returned to Pittsburgh in 1824 to teach and to accept portrait commissions. Bound for Europe in 1827, Lambdin met Rubens Peale in New York City. Peale was the director of the Peale Museum, one of the country's earliest museums, founded in 1786 in Philadelphia by his father, the artist and naturalist Charles Willson Peale. Lambdin never made it to Europe. Encouraged by Peale and his family's museum, Lambdin returned to Pittsburgh and opened his museum at the corner of Fourth and Market streets.

Lambdin displayed a wide variety of paintings, including his own; Indian artifacts; coral; coins; medals; and North American and foreign birds, bones and fossils.

The Pittsburgh public proved to be a keen audience, but Lambdin's museum lasted only four years. In 1832 he moved to Louisville, Kentucky, to pursue more portrait commissions. He operated the museum there until 1837 when he sold it to paint full time.

Outside of a few commercial art galleries and the activities of the Pittsburgh Art Society, founded in 1873, fine art was rarely displayed in public until Carnegie Institute opened to the public on November 5, 1895.

Carnegie Institute included then as it does now the Carnegie Museum of Art, the Carnegie Museum of Natural History, Carnegie Library and the Music Hall. The institute was Andrew Carnegie's largest philanthropic endeavor at that time. He offered $1 million to build it if the city agreed to spend $40,000 annually to maintain it. All told Carnegie gave $27.7 million to the institute during his lifetime.

The museum's collections of fine art, contemporary art and decorative art are housed in the Sarah Scaife Galleries, which were a gift of the Sarah Mellon Scaife Foundation and the Scaife family. The galleries opened in 1974 and were renovated in 2003.

The Carnegie Museums – which consist of the Carnegie Museum of Art; the Carnegie Museum of Natural History; the Carnegie Science Center; and The Andy Warhol Museum – form the nucleus of Pittsburgh's world-class museums, which include The Frick Art Museum and The Mattress Factory.

The Andy Warhol Museum

117 Sandusky Street, North Side
Founded: 1994
Benefactors/Founding Contributors:
The Andy Warhol Foundation for the Visual Arts, Incorporated; Dia Center for the Arts based in New York and private donations.

The museum's collection includes more than 4,000 works by Warhol, including paintings, drawings, prints, photographs, sculpture and installation. Forty-five of Warhol's films are in the collection, as well as 228 four-minute Screen Tests. The museum houses the artist's archives; his personal collection of collectibles and ephemera; 608 Time Capsules, dated collections of material from the artist's daily life; the full run of Interview magazine, which Warhol founded in 1969; approximately 2,500 audiotapes; and scripts, diaries, and correspondence. The museum also hosts exhibits by artists who push the boundaries of art, just as Warhol did.

March 10, 2006: The Andy Warhol Museum is one of the most popular attractions in the city. Warhol, a Pittsburgh native, is widely considered the most important artist of the second-half of the 20th century.

ANDREW RUSSELL/TRIBUNE-REVIEW

Carnegie Museum of Art

4400 Forbes Avenue, Oakland
Founded: 1895
Benefactors/Founding Contributors:
Andrew Carnegie

Andrew Carnegie envisioned a collection consisting of "the Old Masters of tomorrow." In 1896 he initiated the Carnegie International, a series of exhibitions of contemporary art, and proposed that the museum's collection of paintings be formed through purchases from this series. Carnegie founded what is arguably the first museum of modern art in the United States that contains nearly 32,000 objects in its permanent collection, with approximately 1,800 works on display. The Teenie Harris Archive, acquired in 2003, contains about 80,000 negatives by acclaimed black photographer Charles "Teenie" Harris.

JOE APPEL/TRIBUNE-REVIEW

May 2, 2008: The work in the foreground titled "Mallarme" by Mario Merz is on display at the Carnegie Museum of Art during the 2008 Carnegie International, "Life on Mars."

The Carnegie Museum of Natural History

4400 Forbes Avenue, Oakland
Founded: 1895
Benefactors/Founding Contributors:
Andrew Carnegie

When it opened in 1895, the Carnegie Museum of Natural History displayed a modest collection in three rooms of the Carnegie Library in Oakland. The discovery of "Dippy" changed everything. Carnegie's team of paleontologists discovered an 84-foot-long dinosaur skeleton, nicknamed "Dippy," in Sheep Creek, Montana, in 1899. Its massive size meant the museum needed a new home. The current building opened in 1907. Carnegie paid for fossil digs for more than 20 years, producing a world-class collection. Over the years, the museum has added special galleries and halls devoted to gems, geology, mammals, fossils, African wildlife, ancient Egypt and American Indians. The museum, considered one of the best in the country, has a collection of more than 22 million objects and specimens; 50,000 are regularly displayed.

February 26, 2008: This Tyrannosaurus rex was cleaned and reassembled for the Carnegie Museum of Natural History's "Dinosaurs in their Time" exhibit, which shows dinosaurs in more natural and scientifically accurate poses.

JAMES KNOX/TRIBUNE-REVIEW

September 29, 2006: Don't look down! An optical illusion at the Carnegie Science Center creates the impression of being hundreds of feet in the air.

July 20, 2007: Interactive exhibits at the Children's Museum of Pittsburgh allow kids to have fun while learning about art, theater, mechanics and nature. This exhibit is called the Limb Bender.

KEITH HODAN/TRIBUNE-REVIEW

Children's Museum of Pittsburgh

10 Children's Way,
North Side
Founded: 1983
Benefactors/Founding Contributors: *The Junior League of Pittsburgh*

The Children's Museum of Pittsburgh began in the basement of the historic former Post Office building on the North Side. It has expanded twice, once in 1985 and again in 2007. Exhibits include: The Studio, The Attic, The Garage/Workshop, The Theater, Waterplay, The Nursery, Mister Rogers and The Backyard – all of which teach children about art, mechanics, theater, water and nature. "Welcome to Mister Rogers' Neighborhood" was produced in 1998 as a life-sized re-creation of the television show. It was a traveling exhibit until 2004 when it became a permanent fixture in the Children's Museum.

ANDREW RUSSELL/TRIBUNE-REVIEW

The Carnegie Science Center

One Allegheny Avenue, North Side
Founded: 1991
Benefactors/Founding Contributors: *Andrew Carnegie; Henry Buhl Jr., a prosperous Allegheny merchant, who bequeathed money to create The Henry Buhl Jr. Planetarium and Institute of Popular Science.*

The Carnegie Science Center aims to inspire and entertain through exhibits that make science and technology cool. It was honored in 2003 with the National Award for Museum Service by first lady Laura Bush. The science center is the product of fusing the Carnegie Institute and the Buhl Planetarium and Institute of Popular Science. In the 1980s, Buhl Planetarium was looking to expand out of its 1939-era building in Allegheny Center, but it would need additional staffing. It merged with the Carnegie Institute. Ground was broken for the Carnegie Science Center on October 5, 1989. It opened two years later.

KEITH HODAN/TRIBUNE-REVIEW

The Fort Pitt Block House

Point State Park
Founded: 1895
Benefactors/Founding Contributors: *Mary Schenley; the Daughters of the American Revolution*

The Block House, built in 1764, was used as a military structure, trading post and private residence before it was acquired by the DAR, which renovated it and turned it into a museum. It opened to the public on July 15, 1895, making it the oldest continuously operating museum in Pittsburgh. It charges no admission. Visitors can examine the building's original architecture and artifacts, such as musket balls, thimbles and pottery pieces, that were found during archaeological excavations.

The Frick Art Museum at The Frick Art & Historical Center

7227 Reynolds Street,
Point Breeze
Founded: 1970
Benefactors/Founding Contributors:
Helen Clay Frick

Helen Clay Frick was a passionate art collector like her father, Henry Clay Frick, who amassed a large collection of fine and decorative European art. Though she lived much of her adult life between her farm in Bedford, New York, and the family home Eagle Rock at Prides Crossing, Massachusetts, she built The Frick Art Museum in 1969 on the grounds of the family's first home, Clayton, in Point Breeze. The museum opened to the public in 1970. Here visitors will find Renaissance and French 18th-century paintings, porcelains, bronzes, and rare examples of 17th- and 18th-century furniture. The permanent collection includes a portrait by Rubens, a pastoral scene by Boucher, and Italian panel paintings by Giovanni de Paolo and Sassetta.

In 1981, Helen Clay Frick returned to Clayton to live full time. She died there in 1984, leaving provisions for Clayton to be restored and opened to the public. It opened in 1990.

August 26, 2004: Frick Art & Historical Center.

June 21, 2008: The Parade of Champions inside the Heinz History Center

The Mattress Factory

500 Sampsonia Way, North Side
Founded: 1977
Benefactors/Founding Contributors:
Barbara Luderowski and Michael Olijnyk

The museum specializes in installation art – art created for a specific site, often all encompassing, room-sized artworks. It was the first of its kind in the country where artists could create new works with total support and exhibit them to a wide audience. Except for a handful of permanent installations, the Mattress Factory invites artists to work in residence to create a new, site-specific installation. Artists receive lodging, a daily living allowance and all the materials and assistance they require. Since 1982, the museum has presented new works by more than 350 artists.

STEVEN ADAMS/TRIBUNE-REVIEW

October 27, 2001: "Fall" by Tom Bedger was part of "Gestures: An Exhibition of Small Site-Specific Works" at the Mattress Factory.

The Senator John Heinz History Center

1212 Smallman Street,
Strip District
Founded: 1879
Benefactors/Founding Contributors:
Historical Society of Western Pennsylvania, which was founded by William Rinehart, William M. Gormly, and John Fullerton

The Senator John Heinz History Center is the largest history museum in Pennsylvania. The collection was started by the historical society in 1879 to preserve the stories, archives, photographs and objects that tell Pittsburgh's history. The historical society had several homes before moving to the Strip District. In 1895 it moved its archives into the Carnegie Library of Pittsburgh in Oakland. By 1914, it had enough money to move to its own building on Bigelow Boulevard, where it stayed until the Heinz History Center opened in 1996. The history center has seven floors and 200,000 square feet of space. In 2000, it became an affiliate of the Smithsonian Institution. In 2004, it opened the Western Pennsylvania Sports Museum. The history center is named for United States Senator John Heinz, who died in 1991 with six others in an airplane crash near Philadelphia.

91

ARCHITECTURE

The Allegheny County Courthouse and Jail, Downtown, were designed by architect H. H. Richardson in 1883 and built from 1884 to 1888. Richardson died before the buildings were completed. The jail closed in 1995 and now houses the juvenile and family sections of the Common Pleas Court.

Burke's Building at 209 Fourth Avenue, was constructed in 1836 and is the oldest business building in the Golden Triangle. It was designed by John Chislett, an English-trained architect who opened his practice in Pittsburgh in 1833.

The Cathedral of Learning in Oakland took 11 years to complete. It was the brainchild of John Gabbert Bowman, who became the University of Pittsburgh's chancellor in 1921. Bowman and architect Charles Zeller Klauder could not agree on a design for the cathedral. One evening, according to Bowman, he and the architect were listening to the "Magic Fire Music" from the opera "Die Walkure," and Bowman decided that's how he wanted the cathedral to look – climax building on climax, with the building's levels climbing higher and higher. Soon after, Klauder produced the cathedral's design.

The David L. Lawrence Convention Center, named for the former Pittsburgh mayor, opened Downtown in September 2003. About 75 percent of the convention center's exhibition space is lit by natural daylight using windows and skylights. The cantilevered roof was inspired by the three suspension bridges that connect the North Side with Downtown.

The Fort Pitt Block House was built in 1764 by Colonel Henry Bouquet. It stood outside the walls of Fort Pitt as a defensive structure. It is the oldest authenticated building in Western Pennsylvania and the only structure to survive from the fort. It was presented to the Daughters of the American Revolution in 1894 by Mary Schenley. In the early 1900s, Henry Clay Frick wanted to move it to Schenley Park so he could develop the Point. The DAR refused. After a fierce court battle, the state Supreme Court sided with the organization. The Block House sits on its original spot, now inside Point State Park.

The John Woods House in Hazelwood was built in 1792. Woods, the first surveyor of Pittsburgh and Allegheny County, was a state senator in 1797 and elected to the 14th Congress in 1815. He died in 1817 at age 55. Composer Stephen Foster was a frequent visitor to the two-story stone home, often entertaining the Woods family and their guests by playing guitar or piano.

Manchester, in the North Side, merged with Allegheny City in 1867. Many old buildings remain. In 1966, the Pittsburgh History & Landmarks Foundation worked with neighborhood residents to create the first historic preservation district in the nation that was primarily for a black neighborhood. The work is now continued by the Manchester Citizens Corporation.

Mellon Arena, originally the Civic Arena, was built in 1961 to house the Civic Light Opera. Its design features the largest retractable, stainless steel dome in the world. The dome is designed to open and close in just two minutes. The Beatles, Elvis Presley and Frank Sinatra have played there, and the arena has been home to the Pittsburgh Penguins since 1967.

The Mexican War Streets sit in a 27-acre area on Pittsburgh's North Side that was laid out in 1848 by General William Robinson, who had just returned from the Mexican War, as the Buena Vista Extension. The Pittsburgh History & Landmarks Foundation named the area the Mexican War Streets in the late 1960s and started a neighborhood restoration program that became the first in the nation to benefit a mixed-income, integrated neighborhood.

The Neill Log House in Schenley Park was built around 1790 and is one of the few surviving 18th-century structures in Pittsburgh. In 1968, it was restored by the Pittsburgh History & Landmarks Foundation and was outfitted with pioneer furnishings provided by the Junior League of Pittsburgh.

Union Station – Pennsylvania Station Rotunda: It took five years for Union Station, Downtown, to be constructed. The building's rotunda was built in 1900. After the Pennsylvania Railroad went bankrupt, long-distance buses began to use the rotunda as a station and were able to drive under the rotunda's smallest arches. In 1988, Union Station reopened as The Pennsylvanian Residential Apartments and Corporate Homes.

The Union Trust Building, Grant Street and Fifth Avenue, was constructed from 1915 to 1917 as one of Henry Clay Frick's building speculations in the Triangle. When it was built, Union Trust had space for 240 shops and about 700 offices. It underwent a partial restoration in the late 1980s.

KEITH HODAN/TRIBUNE-REVIEW

2008: The Cathedral of Learning is 535 feet high.

2008: The rotunda of The Pennsylvanian, formerly Pennsylvania Station, on Grant Street, Downtown, is open and yet has a cave-like quality.

2006: The Union Trust Building is one of the most striking structures in the city because of its steeply pitched mansard roof. Terra-cotta dormers and ornaments decorate the roof – giving it the appearance of a cathedral – above which rise two, chapel-like mechanical towers. Architect Frederick Osterling designed the building in the Flemish-Gothic style and organized the interior around a central rotunda capped by a stained-glass dome. The Union Trust building was constructed on the site of Pittsburgh's second Saint Paul Cathedral. The third cathedral is in Oakland.

2008: The Allegheny County Courthouse and Jail, considered to be Henry Hobson Richardson's architectural masterpiece, was completed in 1888.

2008: The Burke's Building survived the Great Fire of 1845.

2006: Early morning light illuminates The Inn On The Mexican War Streets.

REGION

Old Economy, Beaver County
Harmony, Butler County

Both run by the Harmonists. Established by followers of Separatist George Rapp in the early 1800s, the villages are early examples of the mix of manufacturing and agriculture in a closed environment. The Harmonists created and developed technology and used it as a competitive edge in the early American economy, particularly in textile manufacturing and agricultural production. In 1814, the Harmonists left Harmony, which still maintains a charming 19th-century village diamond, and moved to Indiana. In 1824, the society settled in Beaver County. The historic site at Old Economy Village, run today by the Pennsylvania Historical and Museum Commission, contains 17 restored structures and a garden built between 1824 and 1830.

Fallingwater, Fayette County

Perhaps the most famous structure designed by Frank Lloyd Wright, Fallingwater was designed as a vacation home for Edgar and Lilianne Kaufmann. Edgar Kaufmann was the owner of Kaufmann's Department Store, and his wife was the president of Montefiore Hospital. The house was constructed over a waterfall and completed in 1938. It was featured that year on the cover of Time magazine. It has been maintained since 1963 by the Western Pennsylvania Conservancy as part of the conservancy's 5,000-acre Bear Run Nature Reserve in Fayette County. More than 100,000 people visit the home annually.

Hopwood, Fayette County

Founded by Virginian John Hopwood in 1791, the village in southern Fayette County was an important stop on the National Road, later Route 40, and its rich history is evident today with more surviving stone buildings than any other community along the road. The National Road was completed in 1818 from Cumberland, Maryland, to Wheeling in what is now West Virginia and allowed for population expansion to the West.

BARRY REEGER/TRIBUNE-REVIEW

March 19, 2008: Blacksmith Randy Wilkins demonstrates his trade in the Blacksmith Shop at Old Economy Village.

Kentuck Knob, Fayette County

Seven miles from Fallingwater is Frank Lloyd Wright's Kentuck Knob, built in 1956 for I.N. and Bernadine Hagan, friends of the Kaufmann family. The Hagans made their fortune managing an ice cream company and lived in the home for 30 years. It is privately owned and has been open to the public since 1996. Kentuck Knob is constructed of cypress, glass and sandstone, with a copper roof. The home was commissioned when Wright was 86 and working on designs for the Guggenheim Museum in New York City.

SEAN STIPP/TRIBUNE-REVIEW

April 16, 2004: The main living room is one of the most impressive rooms at Kentuck Knob, a home designed by Frank Lloyd Wright that has been designated a National Historic Landmark.

Nemacolin Castle, Fayette County

Nemacolin Castle was built in stages between 1789 and 1900 by several generations of the Jacob Bowman family in Brownsville. The 22-room castle features a three-story octagonal tower and a squared third-story tower room. Jacob Bowman operated a trading post at the site and was named commissary to government troops during the Whiskey Rebellion. In 1795, he was commissioned justice of the peace and was named Brownsville's first postmaster by President George Washington. The castle, owned by the county and maintained by the Brownsville Historical Society, is a museum.

Greene County Courthouses

Built in 1796 in Waynesburg, the first courthouse, a two-story log cabin, is the home of the Greene County Historical Society. It was restored and re-dedicated in 2002. The present courthouse was built in 1850. In 1997 a $4 million project included removal of the original jail and sheriff's office and installation of a second courtroom, judge's chambers, law library, and other offices. The project also included renovations to the original courthouse with an attempt to maintain its historical integrity.

National Bank of the Commonwealth

The bank took over the vintage Indiana County Courthouse at Sixth and Philadelphia streets when the county vacated the building in 1970. Designed in the Second Empire style by J.W. Drum, it was constructed in 1870 at a cost of $186,000 on the site of the first courthouse. The restoration work earned an "excellence in design-extended use" award from the Pittsburgh chapter of the American Institute of Architects and Masonry Institute of Western Pennsylvania.

April 15, 2006: The Brownsville Historical Society conducts many events at Nemacolin Castle in Brownsville including this Easter parade.

The David Bradford House, Washington County

Bradford was one of the leading lawyers and politicians of the area, serving as deputy attorney general for Washington County and as a delegate to the Whiskey Rebellion conferences in 1791 and 1792. Built in 1788, the home reflects his high social standing and features a mahogany staircase and interior wood finishes. The stone for the exterior was quarried near Washington. The home is owned by the Pennsylvania Historical and Museum Commission and is managed by volunteers for the Bradford House Historical Association.

TRIBUNE-REVIEW

Brush Hill, Westmoreland County

This privately owned home in Irwin, Westmoreland County, was built in 1798 by Colonel John Irwin, first member of the Irwin family to settle in the region. The National Historic site is considered the first 'mansion-scale' house west of the Allegheny Mountains. Since 1977, Brush Hill has been under the care of owners Don and Dilly Miller, who have restored the stone mansion. It features two-foot-thick walls and hand-hewn oak beams supporting the floors. The home, which is on the National Register of Historic Places, is not open for public tours.

West Overton, Westmoreland County

West Overton is an agriculture village founded by Henry Overholt in 1800 and expanded by his son, Abraham, on Route 819 near Scottdale in Westmoreland County. It is the birthplace of Pittsburgh industrialist Henry Clay Frick. It is believed to be the only intact, pre-Civil War, rural industrial village in Pennsylvania. West Overton features an 1800s distillery, gristmill and the largest brick barn in the state. It is managed by the West Overton Museums board of directors.

Westmoreland County Courthouse

Located on Main Street in downtown Greensburg, the four-story building was erected in 1906. Its central dome, 175 feet above the ground, is of Italian Renaissance style, one of only two in the world designed by the courthouse's original architect, William Kauffman. The structure cost $1.5 million to construct and furnish.

December 26, 2007: Colonel John Irwin's Brush Hill home was decked for the holidays by its owners, Don and Dilly Miller.

1906: Pittsburgh Symphony Orchestra; Emil Paur, conductor, Luigi von Kunitz, concertmaster.

November 19, 1933: George Gershwin sells the first ticket ever sold on a Sunday in Pennsylvania for a concert by the Pittsburgh Symphony Orchestra. Left to right: Mrs. Wilson Maclay Hall, president of the Pittsburgh Symphony Society; Leo Lehman, Pittsburgh businessman who bought the first ticket for $50; Gershwin and Antonio Modarelli, conductor.

SYMPHONY

The Pittsburgh Symphony is an internationally recognized, world-class ensemble. It traces its lineage to the Pittsburgh Orchestra, founded in 1896 with celebrated composer and cellist Victor Herbert, who was music director from 1898 to 1904.

The orchestra was disbanded in 1910, but re-established in 1926. German conductor Otto Klemperer helped reorganize it in 1937-38, but the arrival of the demanding, uncompromising Fritz Reiner in 1938 transformed it.

Reiner left in 1948, and after four years of transition, William Steinberg served as music director from 1952 to 1976. His warm and knowing musicianship elevated the orchestra to international standing. In 1971 Heinz Hall opened as the orchestra's home.

Andre Previn assumed the Heinz Hall podium in 1976, enhancing the orchestra's reputation with the Public Broadcasting Service television series "Previn and the Pittsburgh."

Leonard Bernstein declared the Pittsburgh Symphony "world class" in 1984. Lorin Maazel raised its standing within the elite rank of orchestras, first as music adviser starting in 1986 and then as music director from 1988 to 1996. While reaching much higher technical standards, Maazel and the orchestra also achieved complete fluency in the widest array of international styles.

Mariss Jansons, music director from 1997 to 2005, brought more spontaneity to the music making. Manfred Honeck became music director in September 2008.

BALLET

Pittsburgh Ballet Theatre was founded in 1969 by choreographer Nicholas Petrov at what is now Point Park University. The company took its first steps at Pittsburgh Playhouse and moved to Heinz Hall after it opened in 1971. A full-length production of Sergei Prokofiev's "Romeo and Juliet" was one of Petrov's most ambitious productions.

John Giplin took over the troupe briefly in 1977, followed by Patrick Franz, but the company took its most decisive step in 1982 by engaging Patricia Wilde as artistic director. A star of legendary choreographer George Balanchine's New York City Ballet from 1950 to 1965, Wilde raised Pittsburgh Ballet Theatre to national stature during her 15-year tenure. She highlighted many Balanchine masterpieces and encouraged new choreographers – all the while refining the technical finesse of the company.

Terrence S. Orr succeeded Wilde in 1997. A former principal dancer and ballet master of American Ballet Theatre, Orr blends classic and modern repertoire and encourages exuberant, expressive performances.

The 2002 new production of "The Nutcracker" is his signature creation, set in a historic home in Shadyside. His commissions have boldly embraced modern themes and featured music by such popular artists as Bruce Springsteen, Paul Simon, Cole Porter, Billy Strayhorn and B.E. Taylor.

HEIDI MURRIN/TRIBUNE-REVIEW

December 5, 2002: Members of the Pittsburgh Ballet Theatre rehearse "The Nutcracker" at the Benedum Center.

OPERA

Pittsburgh Opera was founded in 1939 by five women who presented "The Tales of Hoffmann" as its first production on March 15, 1940, at Carnegie Music Hall in Oakland.

Viennese conductor Richard Karp took the artistic helm in 1942. He brought a wide range of repertoire to life with demanding standards and increasingly impressive casts, first at Carnegie Music Hall, after 1945 in the former Syria Mosque, Oakland, and starting in 1971 Heinz Hall,

Downtown.

When Karp died in 1977, Pittsburgh Opera treaded water until 1983 when New York City Opera's Tito Capobianco became artistic director. His tenure began strongly with innovative staging and introduction of "Op-Trans" projected English translation. The company moved to the Benedum Center in 1987, but had recurring financial shortfalls and weaker casts.

In 1997, new Executive Director Mark Weinstein began restoring financial

stability. He became general director in 2000, with Christopher Hahn as artistic director and John Mauceri as music director. Hahn brought stronger casts of singers, adventuresome stagings and integrated modern operas into the repertoire. Mauceri transformed the orchestra with acute stylistic awareness. Mauceri was succeeded by Antony Walker in 2007.

After Weinstein left the Pittsburgh Opera at the end of January 2008, Hahn was named general director.

AIMEE OBIDZINSKI/TRIBUNE-REVIEW

October 22, 2005: Michael Hendrick as Bacchus and Jane Eaglen as Ariadne perform during "Ariadne Auf Naxos" for opening night of the Pittsburgh Opera at the Benedum Center.

January 23, 2008: The Pittsburgh Public Theatre opened n 1975 at the Hazlett Theater on the North Side. In 1999 it moved to the O'Reilly Theatre in the Downtown Cultural District.

THEATER

Even before Pittsburgh was a city and the United States was a nation, there was theater in Pittsburgh.

As early as 1765, a German doctor noted, plays, concerts and comedies were being performed inside Fort Pitt.

The first commercial theater – The New Theatre over the Allegheny – began performances in 1795. More theaters began opening, amateur groups sprouted and Pittsburgh became a regular stop for touring companies.

In 1813 Pittsburgh got its first free-standing theater building – The Theatre on Third Street – near the present day intersection of Third Avenue and Smithfield Street.

By the 1860s more than a dozen theaters were operating around Penn and Liberty Avenues.

The first professional German language theater group debuted in 1863.

In the 1870s several local black theater companies were producing popular melodramas as well as all-black productions of "Macbeth." The first hometown Jewish theater group was founded in 1895 by German Jews.

The 20th century saw the founding of professional theater companies that endure to the present in one form or another.

The influential Pittsburgh Playhouse, now operated by Point Park University,

was founded in 1933. Pittsburgh Civic Light Opera began its first musical theater season in 1946 with "Naughty Marietta" at Pitt Stadium. The Pittsburgh Public Theater debuted in 1975.

Also begun in 1975 was City Players, a program of the City's Parks and Recreation, that became City Theatre Company when it morphed into an independent theater group in 1979.

Additional theater choices include national touring shows presented by PNC Broadway Across America – Pittsburgh, the Pittsburgh Playwrights Theatre Company, Kuntu Repertory, barebones productions, Bricolage, Quantum Theatre and Pittsburgh Irish & Classical Theatre.

PERFORMERS

Frank Gorshin

Being cast as The Riddler in the 1960s television show "Batman" brought stardom to impressionist Gorshin, whose claim to fame up to then was that he was the act that followed the Beatles on "The Ed Sullivan Show." Gorshin was born April 15, 1933, and raised in Pittsburgh. He had dozens of movie and TV credits and starred in an acclaimed one-man show, "Say Goodnight Gracie," about comedian George Burns. He died May 17, 2005, and his tombstone in Calvary Cemetery features a question mark that follows the inscription, "What does it all Mean?"

Martha Graham

She was a pioneer in modern dance who was born on May 11, 1894, in Allegheny City, now the North Side. Graham's bold, angular style was based on movement used during American Indian religious ceremonies and incorporated bare, flexed feet and long leg extensions. In 1926, she founded the Martha Graham Dance Company, which is the oldest contemporary dance company in the world. Graham appeared in most of her choreography well into her 70s. A young lady named Betty Bloomer danced with the company in 1938. She would become first lady Betty Ford. Graham died April 1, 1991, in Spain.

CARL VAN VECHTEN/LIBRARY OF CONGRESS

1961: Martha Graham and Bertram Ross in "Visionary recital."

Michael Keaton

Keaton starred in such films as "Night Shift," "Beetlejuice," "Batman," "Batman Returns" and "Jack Frost." He got his start on "Mr. Rogers' Neighborhood." He has always kept close ties with Pittsburgh, advocating for the Parental Stress Center and appearing on "Mister Rogers' Neighborhood." In 1986 he portrayed a Pittsburgh steelworker in the movie "Gung Ho," which was filmed in the area. Keaton's real name is Michael Douglas. He was born on September 5, 1951, and grew up in Robinson.

Gene Kelly

Kelly brought masculinity and grace to the American movie musical with his dancing. He gave legendary performances in "An American in Paris" and "Singin' in the Rain," which he co-directed. He was born on August 23, 1912, and raised in East Liberty. He graduated from Peabody High School and earned an economics degree from the University of Pittsburgh in 1933. He appeared on Broadway in "The Time of Your Life," and "Pal Joey," which made him a star and led to a movie contract. He died on February 2, 1996, in California. The Pittsburgh Civic Light Opera honors Kelly every year in the Gene Kelly Awards for Excellence in High School Musical Theater, a Tony Awards-style showcase of Allegheny County high school musicals.

AP IMAGES

1952: Gene Kelly in an iconic pose from the motion picture "Singin' in the Rain."

Shirley Jones

After winning the Miss Pittsburgh Pageant in 1952, Jones came in as first runner-up for Miss Pennsylvania and won an apprenticeship to the Pittsburgh Playhouse. In 1953, Rodgers and Hammerstein cast her as a replacement in the chorus of the Broadway production of "South Pacific." She starred in the film versions of "Oklahoma!" as Laurey and as Marian in Meredith Wilson's "The Music Man." She also starred in the television show "The Partridge Family" in the 1970s. She won her Academy Award for Best Supporting Actress in 1960 as Lulu Baines in "Elmer Gantry." Jones was born on March 31, 1934, in Charleroi.

Rob and Kathleen Marshall

Brother and sister, the Marshalls grew up in Squirrel Hill, and got their start playing von Trapp children in the 1973 Pittsburgh Civic Light Opera production of "The Sound of Music." Rob, born October 17, 1960, directed the movie musical, "Chicago," which won the Academy Award for best picture for 2002. He was also nominated for best director. He directed "Memoirs of a Geisha," which won three Academy Awards for 2005. Kathleen, born in 1962, is a two-time Tony Award-winner for choreography.

Dennis Miller

Miller got his start on KDKA's "Evening Magazine" and became a star as the sardonic "Saturday Night Live" anchor for the "Weekend Update" sketch. He won five Emmys for his talk show, "Dennis Miller Live" on HBO. He worked as a commentator for ABC's "Monday Night Football." In 2007 he started "The Dennis Miller Show" on radio. Miller was born November 3, 1953, and grew up in Castle Shannon. He graduated from what is now Point Park University with a major in journalism.

LYNN JOHNSON

Fred Rogers was inducted into the Television Hall of Fame in 1999.

Fred Rogers

He brought his young viewers into the Land of Make Believe as creator and host of the four-time Emmy Award-winning PBS television program "Mister Rogers' Neighborhood." Rogers started entertaining and teaching children through television in 1953 with the show "The Children's Corner." He made his on-camera debut in Toronto, as host of "Mister Rogers." He returned to Pittsburgh where "Mister Rogers' Neighborhood" debuted two years later. It has aired nationally since 1968 and runs in syndication. Rogers was ordained a minister by the Pittsburgh Presbytery in 1962. He was born in Latrobe on March 20, 1928, and died in Pittsburgh on February 17, 2003.

LIBRARY OF CONGRESS

Lillian Russell is buried in Allegheny Cemetery.

David O. Selznick

A movie producer during Hollywood's Golden Age, Selznik brought "Gone With the Wind" to life, winning an Oscar for Best Picture for 1939. A Selznick film, "Rebecca," also picked up the Best Picture award for 1940. Selznick was born in Pittsburgh on May 10, 1902. He died June 22, 1965, in Hollywood.

Jimmy Stewart

Stewart won the Academy Award for Best Actor for 1940 for "The Philadelphia Story," but he is best remembered as the star of "It's a Wonderful Life," a Christmas staple, portraying the suicidal George Bailey, who realizes he has blessed the lives of his friends and family. Stewart appeared in 55 films from the 1930s through the 1990s. In 1972, he hosted "The Jimmy Stewart Show." Stewart was a bomber pilot during World War II who refused special treatment and completed 25 missions over Europe. He is the pride of Indiana, Pennsylvania, where he was born May 20, 1908. He died in Hollywood on July 2, 1997.

Lillian Russell

A singer and actress, Russell was known as the most famous beauty of the late 19th century. Russell was a women's rights activist. The play "Hearts and Ziamonds" was written about her and Willa Cather, an author who lived in Pittsburgh at the same time. Russell was born December 4, 1861, in Iowa. In 1912, she married Alexander Moore, editor of the Pittsburgh Leader and spent her last years in Pittsburgh, where she died June 6, 1922.

Sharon Stone

The woman who once described herself as a nerdy, ugly duckling became a sensation with the racy interrogation scene in the film, "Basic Instinct." Stone received an Academy Award nomination for Best Actress for 1995 for her performance in "Casino." Stone was born in Meadville on March 10, 1958, and attended Edinboro University of Pennsylvania.

VISUAL

Charles 'Teenie' Harris

Harris was a photographer whose work captured the heart of urban life in Pittsburgh. Born July 2, 1908, in the Hill District, he told the history of the black community from the 1930s through the 1970s. He worked for 40 years as staff photographer for the Pittsburgh Courier. He lived in Pittsburgh his entire life. The Carnegie Museum of Art acquired Harris' archive in 2003, which contains about 80,000 negatives. He died on June 12, 1998.

JAMES M. KUBUS/TRIBUNE-REVIEW

LIBRARY OF CONGRESS

Mary Cassatt

Cassatt was an Impressionist painter best known for her depictions of women and for the theme of mother and child. She received critical acclaim in a predominantly male profession. Cassatt was born May 22, 1844, in the city of Allegheny, now the North Side, but grew up in Philadelphia. She was a member of the Associated Artists of Pittsburgh, but spent the majority of her adult life in Paris. She died in France on June 14, 1926.

GIFT OF BARBARA M. LAWSON IN MEMORY OF
ROSWELL MILLER JR./CARNEGIE MUSEUM OF ART

Aaron Harry Gorson

Gorson's best-known works capture the drama of Pittsburgh's steel mills as studies of darkness and light. He was born on June 2, 1872, and emigrated from Lithuania in 1888. He settled in Philadelphia, working by day in a clothing factory and studying at night to become a painter. He moved to Pittsburgh to be near his patron and began painting mill scenes. Even after he moved to New York in 1921 and focused on scenes of Manhattan and the Hudson River, he continued to paint the mills of Pittsburgh. He died on October 11, 1933, in New York City.

John Kane

Kane was a self-taught folk artist who was born August 19, 1860, in Scotland and settled in Braddock. He was a house painter and handyman who lost a leg in a rail yard accident. He began painting Pittsburgh landscapes and moved to portraits, religious subjects and scenes of Scotland. His breakthrough occurred in 1927 when his painting, "Scene in the Scottish Highlands," was accepted at the Carnegie International Exhibition. He died August 10, 1934, in Pittsburgh.

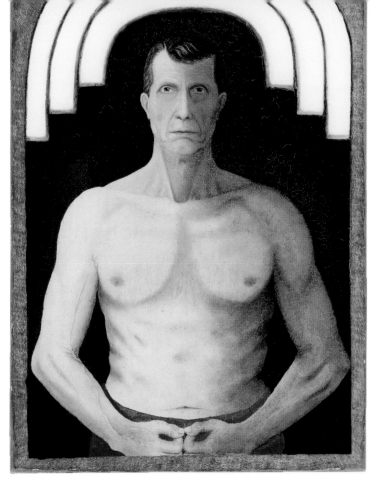

MUSEUM OF MODERN ART, NEW YORK, NY; ABBY ALDRICH ROCKEFELLER FUND;
LICENSED BY SCALA/ART RESOURCE, NEW YORK, NY

Samuel Rosenberg

Rosenberg was a painter whose work spanned almost six decades. His paintings focused on the social and economic conditions of the times, capturing the tone of The Great Depression, World War II, and other cultural and social highs and lows. Rosenberg was born in Pittsburgh on June 28, 1896, and was a professor at Carnegie Mellon University. His Pittsburgh streetscapes were inspired by the Hill District, where he grew up, and by the city's steep hills and crooked landscape. He died on July 23, 1972, in Pittsburgh.

WESTMORELAND MUSEUM OF AMERICAN ART

Andy Warhol

Warhol is the visual artist who turned an image of a Campbell's soup can into priceless art. Warhol's work redefined modern art. He turned everyday commercial products into pop icons. His most famous works include a series of celebrity silk-screen prints featuring Marilyn Monroe, Elvis and countless self-portraits. Warhol was born in Pittsburgh on August 6, 1928, and graduated from Carnegie Mellon University, majoring in pictorial design. His work is housed in the six-floor Andy Warhol Museum, which opened on the North Side in 1994. He died on February 22, 1987, in New York City, suffering a heart attack after gallbladder surgery.

ANDY WARHOL MUSEUM; © 2008 ANDY WARHOL FOUNDATION FOR THE VISUAL ARTS/ARS, NEW YORK

MUSIC

ANDREW RUSSELL/TRIBUNE-REVIEW

April 14, 2007: Christina Aguilera performs at Mellon Arena.

Christina Aguilera

Born December 18, 1980, on Staten Island, New York, pop singer Aguilera moved to Western Pennsylvania in 1987 and graduated from North Allegheny High School 10 years later. Her self-titled debut album, featuring the hit single "Genie in a Bottle," went multi-platinum in 1999. The Grammy-award winning singer, who performed the national anthem before Pittsburgh sporting events as a girl, has sold more than 25 million albums. She sponsors the Women's Center and Shelter of Greater Pittsburgh for battered women and children.

George Benson

A jazz musician born in the Hill District on March 26, 1946, Benson began his musical career playing a cigar-box ukulele on street corners in the Hill District. He later graduated to playing the guitar at local clubs. Benson joined Jack McDuff, another jazz musician, on tour but left in 1965 to form his own group. He released the album "Breezin' " in 1976, and it was the first jazz record to go platinum. Benson has won eight Grammy awards.

Harold Betters

A jazz musician known as Mister Trombone, Betters is a native of Connellsville, born on March 21, 1928. He has played with many jazz greats, including Louis Armstrong and Al Hurt and once toured with Ray Charles. He has recorded 18 albums. The Encore in Shadyside was known as "The House that Betters Built."

Johnny Costa

Born in Arnold, January 18, 1922, Costa was a jazz pianist and musician for "Mr. Rogers' Neighborhood," which was taped at WQED-TV in Oakland. Before that, he served as music director at KDKA. Costa lived in Arnold and in New Kensington most of his life. He once toured nationally and was musical director of "The Mike Douglas Show," but abandoned both to return home. He died October 11, 1996, in Arnold.

Perry Como

Born in Canonsburg on May 18, 1912, Como had 50 Top 10 records, three popular weekly television programs and several television specials. His hits include "Till the End of Time," "Don't Let the Stars Get in Your Eyes," "Hot Diggity," "Round and Round," "Catch a Falling Star," "Papa Loves Mambo," "Home for the Holidays" and "It's Impossible." He died May 12, 2001, in Florida, six days before his 89th birthday.

Stephen Foster

Foster, an American composer, was born in Lawrenceville on July 4, 1826. His songs were distinctly American in theme, and he's best known for penning "Oh Susanna," "Camptown Races" and "My Old Kentucky Home." Foster died destitute on January 13, 1864, at the age of 37 in New York City.

HEIDI MURRIN/TRIBUNE-REVIEW

December 2, 2004: Joe Grushecky, and members of The Houserockers band jam with Bruce Springsteen during the Concert for Flood Aid 2004.

Joe Grushecky

Grushecky, born on May 6, 1948, in Greensburg, is a singer and songwriter who has worked out of Pittsburgh for more than 25 years. He has worked extensively with Bruce Springsteen, who briefly joined Grushecky's band as a guitar player for a club tour in the early 1990s. Joe Grushecky and the Houserockers released their first album in 1979, and Grushecky released his first solo album in 2002. In 2004, he organized "Flood Aid," a concert to help local victims of Hurricane Ivan that raised $265,000 for the Salvation Army.

Walt Harper

Harper was born in 1926 and grew up in Schenley Heights. A jazz pianist and nightclub owner, he played at Crawford's Grill in the Hill District and recorded several albums. He owned two Pittsburgh jazz clubs, Walt Harper's Attic and Harper's Jazz Club. He died October 25, 2006, in Pittsburgh.

Victor Herbert

Herbert was born in Dublin, Ireland, on February 1, 1859. He was a composer and conductor who led the Pittsburgh Symphony Orchestra from 1898 to 1904. In 1895, he wrote "The Belle of Pittsburgh March," but he was best known for his operettas, including "Babes in Toyland" and "Naughty Marietta." He also wrote music for some of the Ziegfeld Follies. He died May 26, 1924, in New York City.

LIBRARY OF CONGRESS

Pittsburgh Symphony Orchestra Conductor Victor Herbert studies a score. His enthusiasm inspired his musicians and audiences.

Earl "Fatha" Hines

Hines was a jazz pianist, who was born in Duquesne on December 28, 1903. He graduated from Schenley High School. He played piano in big bands and later joined Louis Armstrong's quintet in Chicago. He originated the "trumpet style" of piano playing, in which he produced hornlike solo lines on octaves with his right hand and the harmony with his left. He died April 22, 1983, in California.

Lena Horne

A singer, dancer and actress who performed in movies, New York nightclubs and on Broadway, Horne won a special Tony Award for her one-woman show, "Lena Horne: The Lady and Her Music." She was born in Brooklyn, New York, on June 30, 1917, but lived for a short time in Pittsburgh during her brief marriage to Louis Jones, with whom she had two children. She has been active in the civil rights movement.

PHILIP G. PAVELY/TRIBUNE-REVIEW

October 21, 1999: Marvin Hamlisch, principal pops conductor for the Pittsburgh Symphony Orchestra, considers music an international language that can bring people together.

Marvin Hamlisch

The Broadway composer became the Pittsburgh Symphony Orchestra's principal Pops conductor in 1995. Born June 2, 1944, Hamlisch is a quick-witted host who frequently showcases the inexhaustible riches of American musicals. "A Chorus Line" won him a Tony in 1975, and the first Pulitzer Prize in Drama for a musical in 15 years. A big Pirates fan, Hamlisch often converses from stage with individuals in the audience, especially children.

PHILIP G. PAVELY/TRIBUNE-REVIEW

August 7, 2004: On stage, Donnie Iris is a star. Back home in Beaver Falls, he says, he's just another name on a mailbox.

Donnie Iris

Born Dominic Ierace on February 28, 1943, Iris grew up in Ellwood City and has lived in Beaver Falls most of his life. Iris co-founded and fronted The Jaggerz, a Pittsburgh band that had a national hit single, "The Rapper," written and sung by Iris, in 1970. Later, Iris joined with Mark Avsec and three other musicians to form Donnie Iris and the Cruisers. Their song "Ah! Leah!" hit 29th on the Billboard's Top 100 pop chart.

Ahmad Jamal

Jamal, a jazz musician, was born on July 2, 1930, and raised in Pittsburgh. He began to play the piano at age 3 and started formal training at 7. Jamal was on the road at 17 and composing noteworthy songs four years later. One of them, "New Rhumba," eventually was recorded by jazz legend Miles Davis. Jamal has performed at Carnegie Hall in New York City.

Henry Mancini

The Academy Award-winning composer was born in Cleveland on April 16, 1924, and grew up in Aliquippa. Mancini created scores for television shows and films, including "Peter Gunn," "Breakfast at Tiffany's" and "The Pink Panther." He recorded more than 90 albums. He died June 14, 1994, in California. In April 2004, Mancini was honored by the United States Postal Service with a commemorative stamp.

Lorin Maazel

He was born March 6, 1930, in France to American parents. When his violin teacher came to Pittsburgh to accept a position with the Pittsburgh Symphony, the Maazel family followed. He entered the University of Pittsburgh in 1947 to study philosophy, languages and mathematics. While a student, Maazel was a violinist with the symphony and an apprentice conductor. He quickly established himself as a major conductor and served as music director for the Pittsburgh Symphony from 1988 to 1996 and now serves as music director of the New York Philharmonic, the oldest symphony orchestra in the United States.

Joe Negri

Born June 10, 1930, Negri is a jazz guitarist known for his role as Handyman Negri on "Mister Rogers' Neighborhood." He grew up on Mount Washington and attended South Hills High School and Carnegie Mellon University. He served as musical director at WTAE for 20 years and now teaches jazz guitar at the University of Pittsburgh, Duquesne University and CMU.

SIDNEY DAVIS/TRIBUNE-REVIEW

March 18, 2001: Joe Negri began performing as a child and was once chosen as a Pittsburgh Star of Tomorrow. Among his many compositions is a Jazz Mass titled, "The Mass of Hope."

William Steinberg

Steinberg was music director of the Pittsburgh Symphony from 1952 to 1976. He was born August 1, 1899, in Germany but emigrated during the Nazi regime to Palestine where he co-founded the Palestine Symphony Orchestra, which would become the Israel Philharmonic Orchestra. He spent several seasons with the NBC Orchestra and the Buffalo Philharmonic before coming to Pittsburgh. At home in Squirrel Hill, he could be seen tending his garden in spring and summer. He also was music director of the Boston Symphony from 1969 to 1972. He died May 16, 1978, in New York City.

Billy Strayhorn

Strayhorn, a jazz composer and pianist, was born November 29, 1915, in Dayton, Ohio, and was 5 when his family moved to Pittsburgh. He took piano lessons and played in the high school band and wrote a concerto for his graduation from Westinghouse High School. He joined Duke Ellington's band in 1939. After Strayhorn died of cancer on May 31, 1967, Ellington honored him by recording, "And His Mother Called Him Bill," a collection of Strayhorn's compositions.

Stanley Turrentine

A saxophonist who was born on April 22, 1928, Turrentine grew up in the Hill District. He played in the band of Lowell Fulson in the 1950s, moved to Ray Charles' ensemble and then was the tenor player with organist Shirley Scott, to whom he was married for a time. In the 1970s and early 1980s, he crossed over to pop. When he returned to mainstream jazz in the late 1980s, he reclaimed many followers. Despite changes in material, Turrentine never abandoned his rich, soulful tone. He died on September 12, 2000, in New York City.

Bobby Vinton

Vinton has sold more than 75 million records. The singer-songwriter was born April 16, 1935, in Canonsburg, the son of local band leader Stan Vinton. He graduated from Duquesne University with a degree in music composition. Serving in the Army inspired one of his biggest hits, "Mr. Lonely." His song, "My Melody of Love," sung partially in Polish was embraced by Polish-Americans as an unofficial anthem.

Earl Wild

Born in Pittsburgh November 26, 1915, Wild is considered one of the greatest pianists of the 20th century. He was 14 when he was hired to play piano and celeste in the Pittsburgh Symphony Orchestra and has performed with most major orchestras in the world. He served in the United States Navy as a musician in World War II and later worked as a performer, composer and conductor at ABC. He has recorded with more than 20 record labels.

WRITERS & PLAYWRIGHTS

Willa Cather

Students at Allegheny High School in 1901 learned English and poetry from a young woman who would win the Pulitzer Prize in 1923 for her novel, "One of Ours," about World War I. Cather was born in Virginia on December 7, 1873, and grew up on the Nebraska prairie. After graduating from the University of Nebraska, she came to Pittsburgh in 1895 to head Home Monthly magazine. She later worked at the Pittsburgh Daily Leader. Her early fiction and poetry was based in Pittsburgh. In 1906, Cather moved to New York to work at McClure's Magazine before becoming a full-time novelist in 1912. Her many works include "O Pioneers!," and "Death Comes for the Archbishop." She died on April 24, 1947, in New York City.

Michael Chabon

It's the stuff of fiction – unknown writer's first-time novel becomes a blockbuster. But that's exactly what happened to Chabon and his first novel, "The Mysteries of Pittsburgh." Born on May 24, 1963, in Washington, D.C., Chabon studied at Carnegie Mellon University and graduated from the University of Pittsburgh. "The Mysteries of Pittsburgh," published in 1988, was written for his master's thesis at the University of California at Irvine. He followed up with "The Wonder Boys" in 1995, also set in Pittsburgh. Chabon won a Pulitzer Prize in 2001 for his third novel, "The Amazing Adventures of Kavalier & Clay" and published "The Yiddish Policeman's Union" in 2007 to critical acclaim.

J. C. SCHISLER/TRIBUNE-REVIEW

June 3, 2001: Author Michael Chabon, who wrote "The Mysteries of Pittsburgh" while a student at the University of Pittsburgh, was in town to review the script for "Wonder Boys", a movie starring Michael Douglas and Robert Downey, Jr. adapted from Chabon's novel of the same title.

Marcia Davenport

Davenport told of lost love, loyalty, ambition and tragedy within the steelmaking Scott family in her novel, "Valley of Decision," which was set in Pittsburgh. Born on June 9, 1903, in New York City, Davenport lived in Pittsburgh while she researched the book, which was published in 1942. She was a music critic, and she wrote for the New Yorker. She wrote an acclaimed biography of Mozart, published in 1932. She died in California on January 15, 1996.

George S. Kaufman

Kaufman was born in Pittsburgh on November 16, 1889, and started out to become a lawyer, but he dropped out of Western Pennsylvania University, now the University of Pittsburgh, and moved to New York in 1909. He worked as a reporter and attracted some notice as a humorist. In 1917, he joined the New York Times as drama reporter and became drama editor, a position he held until 1930. He wrote 45 Broadway plays, all but one in collaboration with other authors. With Moss Hart, he wrote "You Can't Take It With You," which won the Pulitzer Prize in 1937 and with Morrie Ryskind and George and Ira Gershwin wrote, "Of Thee I Sing," which in 1932 became the first musical to win a Pulitzer Prize. He died in New York City on June 2, 1961.

David McCullough

McCullough, author and historian, was born July 7, 1933, in Pittsburgh and grew up in Point Breeze. His books breathe life into American history. He won a Pulitzer Prize in 2002 for "John Adams" and in 1993 for "Truman." In 2006, he received the Presidential Medal of Freedom, the nation's highest civilian honor. Other books include "The Johnstown Flood," "The Great Bridge" and "The Path between The Seas." McCullough has narrated numerous documentaries, most notably, Ken Burns' epic documentary, "The Civil War."

JOE APPEL/TRIBUNE-REVIEW

April 4, 2008: David McCullough has won two Pulitzer Prizes.

Mary Roberts Rinehart

Roberts was born August 12, 1876, in Allegheny City and studied to be a nurse. She married Doctor Stanley Marshall Rinehart. She became a novelist, playwright and journalist. Her first significant work was "The Circular Staircase," published in 1908. She wrote many short stories and other who-done-its and is considered a master of the genre. She was a war correspondent during World War I. She died on September 22, 1958, in New York City and is buried with her husband, a major in the United States Army Medical Corps, in Arlington National Cemetery.

Gertrude Stein

She was born February 3, 1874, in Allegheny City and moved at age 3 with her family to Vienna and then Paris, finally settling in Oakland, California. Stein studied medicine at Johns Hopkins Medical School, but left without graduating. She became a playwright, poet and novelist. She moved to Paris after World War I to write. She encouraged the talents of artists Pablo Picasso and Henri Matisse and writers F. Scott Fitzgerald and Ernest Hemingway among others. Some of her works include "The Making of Americans," "Autobiography of Alice B. Toklas" and "Three Lives." She died July 27, 1946, in France.

John Edgar Wideman

Wideman has won the prestigious PEN/Faulkner Award for Fiction twice. He was born June 14, 1941, in Washington, D.C., and grew up in Homewood, graduating from Peabody High School and the University of Pennsylvania. He became the second black student to win a Rhodes Scholarship. Three works, "Damballah," "Hidden Place," and "Sent for You Yesterday" – are called the Homewood Trilogy. His memoir, "Brothers and Keepers" is a painful examination of the path that led his younger brother, Robert, to prison for murder and the path that brought him to the heights of contemporary literature.

KEITH HODAN/TRIBUNE-REVIEW

March 26, 1999: August Wilson, winner of a Pulitzer Prize and a Tony Award, poses for a portrait outside the Pittsburgh Public Theatre, on the North Side.

August Wilson

His 10-play cycle chronicled the black experience in 20th century America. All but one, "Ma Rainey's Black Bottom," are set in the Hill District, where Wilson was born on April 27, 1945, and grew up. "Fences" and "The Piano Lesson," each won the Pulitzer Prize. He left school at 15 after a skeptical teacher questioned whether he was the real author of a homework assignment. He educated himself at the Carnegie Library. Soon after, Wilson enlisted in the United States Army, but left after a year, working at jobs that included porter, short-order cook and dishwasher. He was drawn to the theater and in 1978 moved to Saint Paul, Minnesota, where he wrote five plays that would go to Broadway. He settled in Seattle, where he died on October 2, 2005. He once said: "It's somehow harder to do almost anything you want to do in Pittsburgh than it is anywhere else. But, it's who I am. The city of Pittsburgh has molded and shaped me, in large part, to who I am. I cannot divorce myself."

CHAPTER 10

sports

How best to measure Pittsburgh as a sports town?

We could start with the 12 world championships – five each for the Steelers and Pirates, two for the Penguins – and throw in the unbeaten 1976 Pitt Panthers football team, plus some title-winning Pitt teams from much earlier in the 20th century.

The conversation could then roll into how Pittsburgh athletes authored some of the great moments in sports history, such as Bill Mazeroski's World Series-winning home run against the New York Yankees in 1960, Franco Harris' Immaculate Reception against the Oakland Raiders in 1972 and Harvey Haddix's 12 perfect innings against the Milwaukee Braves in 1959.

And that would surely lead us to reminisce about all the legendary figures that have plied their trade in Pittsburgh or sprung from here. Men such as Mario Lemieux, Roberto Clemente, Tony Dorsett, Art Rooney Sr., Dan Marino, Joe Namath, Honus Wagner and Chuck Noll would no doubt spring to mind, followed by dozens of others.

JAMES M. KUBUS/TRIBUNE-R

1997: Artist Judy Penzer's "The Wall of Fame" on the Penzer Building, Downtown, depicted Pittsburgh sports legends Mario Lemieux, Roberto Clemente, Mean Joe Greene, Jack Lambert and Bill Mazeroski. The Penzer Building is gone, demolished for a department store. Piatt Place stands on the site now. Judy Penzer died July 18, 1996, when TWA Flight 800 exploded shortly after takeoff from John F. Kennedy International Airport in New York City.

1992: With the Stanley Cup at center ice, the Penguins watch as their second consecutive championship banner is raised at the Civic Arena.

2008: The Steelers' five Super Bowl trophies are on display at the team headquarters on the South Side.

But to really get a feel for this town's love affair with sports, to accurately gauge the pulse, you need to know about the fans.

You need to go to a game – maybe a Friday night high school football game at the Wolvarena in Turtle Creek, where future Heisman Trophy winner Leon Hart ran wild in the 1940s.

Or maybe you just need to know of nights like December 7, 2006, at Heinz Field, when the Steelers hosted the hated Cleveland Browns in an utterly meaningless late-season affair between two struggling teams.

Meaningless in the standings, that is. In the stands, the game was charged with meaning.

Fans screamed their hearts out on a night described by Steelers radio analyst Craig Wolfley as "colder than a tin toilet in Siberia." Way up in Section 541 – near the top of the stadium, fully exposed to the biting wind – a group huddled together, and a 33-year-old Steelers backer named Chuck Balieu spoke for all of them and all the others when he said, "I wouldn't miss a Steeler game for the world."

If that didn't convince you of Pittsburgh's passion, you could cross town and plop yourself down at Game 6 of the 2008 Stanley Cup final. The strangest thing happened that night, in the immediate aftermath of the Penguins' series-losing, 3-2 defeat to the Detroit Red Wings.

The crowd cheered.

More than 17,000 fans greeted the moment of ultimate heartbreak and bitter defeat with a throaty "Let's Go Pens!" chant, saluting their team for a tremendous season.

To an outsider, the scene might have evoked The Grinch standing stunned as the residents of Whoville celebrated down below, despite losing all their stockings, gifts and trees.

How did the narrator put it in that classic Christmas tale …

He puzzled and puzzled till his puzzler was sore. Then the Grinch thought of something he hadn't before. Maybe Christmas, he thought, doesn't come from a store. Maybe Christmas … perhaps … means a little bit more!

In Pittsburgh, for sure, sports mean a little bit more. Always have and always will.

NEGRO LEAGUES

Color prevented some of the best players in baseball from playing in the American or National leagues.

Catcher Josh Gibson, pitchers Satchel Paige and Martin Dihigo, first baseman Buck Leonard, third baseman Judy Johnson, and outfielders "Cool Papa" Bell and Oscar Charleston spent at least part of their careers in Pittsburgh playing for two successful Negro League franchises, the Pittsburgh Crawfords and the Homestead Grays.

The Pittsburgh Keystones played in the short-lived National Colored Base Ball League, the first organized Negro League, in 1887. The league lasted one week. A second team took the name, Pittsburgh Keystones, in 1922. It lasted one season and went 16-21.

The Crawfords were organized by Gus Greenlee, owner of the Crawford Grill in the Hill District. In 1931, Greenlee, a bootlegger and numbers racketeer, used his gambling profits to buy the team

and build a ballpark with space for 7,000 fans on Bedford Avenue.

Greenlee formed the Negro National League in 1933, and the Crawfords were the powerhouse team for six seasons. However, the team was weakened by player defections, and it moved to Toledo when Greenlee sold the franchise in 1939.

The Grays, formed in 1912, became the next great Negro League dynasty, winning nine straight NNL titles. Cumberland Posey Jr., the son of a prominent Homestead businessman, served as player, manager and owner. The team played in Forbes Field in Oakland.

Gibson, known as the "black Babe Ruth," was the most feared slugger in the league. He played for the Crawfords from 1930 to 1937 and for the Grays from 1937 to 1946.

Gibson died of a stroke in 1947 when he was just 35. Three months later, Jackie Robinson became the first black athlete to play in the major leagues. Integration began to lure the league's best players. The Grays disbanded at the close of the 1950 season. The last Negro League teams folded in the 1960s.

NOTABLE ATHLETES

James T. "Cool Papa" Bell

centerfielder
Homestead Grays: 1932, 1943-46
Pittsburgh Crawfords: 1933-38

Just how fast was he? "Cool Papa Bell was so fast, he could get out of bed, turn out the lights across the room and be back in bed under the covers before the lights went out," Josh Gibson once said. Bell helped the Grays win three Negro League titles from 1942 to 1944. He was recorded to have rounded the bases in 12 seconds. Another story said he scored on a sacrifice fly from second base. Negro League pitcher Satchel Paige noted in his biography, "If colleges had known about Cool Papa, Jesse Owens would have looked like he was walking." Bell was born May 17, 1903, in Starkville, Mississippi and died March 7, 1991, in St. Louis.

Josh Gibson

catcher
Homestead Grays: 1930-31, 1937-39, 1942-46
Pittsburgh Crawfords: 1932-36

Gibson was to the Negro Leagues what Babe Ruth was to Major League Baseball. Sketchy record-keeping has made it difficult to pinpoint how many home runs Gibson hit, but his plaque in the National Baseball Hall of Fame says he hit almost 800. Gibson batted .426 in recorded at bats against big-league pitchers. Gibson died at 35 from a brain tumor, only three months before Jackie Robinson broke the Major Leagues' color barrier. Gibson was born December 21, 1911, in Buena Vista, Georgia, and died January 20, 1947, in Pittsburgh. In 1972, Gibson became the second Negro League player to be enshrined in the Hall of Fame.

Satchel Paige

Pittsburgh Crawfords pitcher 1931-37

Paige, widely considered one of the greatest pitchers to play professional baseball, had a career spanning from 1926 to 1965, playing for Negro League clubs and Major League Baseball teams. Born July 7, 1906, in Mobile, Alabama, he spent six seasons with the Pittsburgh Crawfords, baffling batters with such inventions as the Bat Dodger and the Hesitation Pitch. He joined the Cleveland Indians at age 42 during the 1948 pennant race, becoming the majors' oldest rookie. In 1971, Paige became the first Negro League player to be inducted into the Baseball Hall of Fame. He died June 8, 1982, in Kansas City, Missouri.

CARNEGIE LIBRARY OF PITTSBURGH

1949: From 1937 to 1945 the Homestead Grays won nine straight Negro League pennants.

PIRATES

As the oldest professional franchise in Pittsburgh, the Pirates can trace their roots to the Pittsburgh Alleghenies, who played in 1877 in the minor-league International Association. The team disbanded the following year.

The Alleghenies re-formed in 1882 and joined the American Association, a rival of the National League. When the Kansas City club was booted from the National League after the 1886 season, Pittsburgh was admitted.

In 1891, the Alleghenies signed second baseman Louis Bierbauer, who had played the previous four seasons with the Philadelphia Athletics in the American Association. The A's accused Pittsburgh of "pirating" Bierbauer and the nickname stuck.

The Pirates were National League champs in 1901, '02 and '03, but did not claim a World Series crown until 1909. The seven-game conquest of the Detroit Tigers marked the first of five world championships for Pittsburgh.

The Pirates prevailed again in 1925, defeating the Washington Senators in a seven-game World Series. But it would be 35 years until the franchise won another championship, which occurred in dramatic fashion when Bill Mazeroski's ninth-inning homer upset the New York Yankees, 10-9, in Game 7 of the 1960 World Series. It remains the only Game 7 series-ending home run in baseball history.

The Pirates were a dominant team of the 1970s, winning the World Series against Baltimore in 1971 and 1979.

CARNEGIE LIBRARY OF PITTSBURGH

October 9, 1909: Spectators climb a pole outside Forbes Field to get a better view of the Game 2 of the 1909 World Series. The Pirates lost, 7-2, to the Detroit Tigers but went on to win the series.

2008: The Pirates retired jerseys numbers are displayed at PNC Park.

October 13, 1960: Bill Mazeroski is the only man in Major League Baseball history to hit a home run in the bottom of the ninth inning of a seventh game to win the World Series.

RETIRED JERSEYS

NAME	NUMBER
Billy Meyer *manager, 1948-52*	1
Ralph Kiner	4
Willie Stargell	8
Bill Mazeroski	9
Paul Waner	11
Pie Traynor	20
Roberto Clemente	21
Honus Wagner	33
Danny Murtaugh *manager in four stints from 1957-76*	40
Jackie Robinson *retired throughout all of Major League Baseball*	42

HARRY HARRIS/AP IMAGES

CARNEGIE LIBRARY OF PITTSBURGH

1883: The Alleghenies.

PIRATES IN THE HALL OF FAME

Pirate shortstop Honus Wagner was in the first class inducted into the Baseball Hall of Fame. Since then a dozen Pirates have followed.

Name	Position	Year Inducted	Length of career	Years in Pittsburgh
Max Carey	outfielder	1961	1910-33	1910-26, 1930
Fred Clarke	outfielder and manager	1945	1894-1915	1900-15 (player and manager)
Roberto Clemente	outfielder	1973	1955-72	1955-72
Hazen "Kiki" Cuyler	outfielder	1968	1921-38	1921-27
Barney Dreyfuss	owner	2008	1900-32	1900-32
Ralph Kiner	outfielder	1975	1946-55	1946-53
Bill Mazeroski	second baseman	2001	1956-72	1956-72
Willie Stargell	outfielder and first baseman	1988	1962-82	1962-82
Harold "Pie" Traynor	third baseman and manager	1948	1920-37 (player) 1934-39 (manager)	1920-39
Arky Vaughan	shortstop	1985	1932-48	1932-41
Honus Wagner	shortstop	1936	1897-1917	1900-17
Lloyd Waner	outfielder	1967	1927-43	1927-41
Paul Waner	outfielder	1952	1926-45	1926-40

SOURCE: PITTSBURGH PIRATES

CHAZ PALLA/TRIBUNE-REVIEW

Usher Phil Coyne, 90, has worked in Forbes Field, Three Rivers Stadium and PNC Park.

August 25, 2008: Pedestrians pass by the Legends of Pittsburgh Baseball mural on Ross Street beneath the Boulevard of the Allies.

April 16, 2001: The Pirates' Aramis Ramirez walks to the batter's box with the Downtown skyline in full view. The park is consistently named as one of the best baseball venues in America.

Roberto Clemente made the number 21 synonymous with baseball greatness.

BATTING CHAMPIONSHIPS

The Pirates have won more batting championships than any other team in Major League Baseball.

NAME	YEAR
Honus Wagner (.381)	1900
Ginger Beaumont (.357)	1902
Honus Wagner (.355)	1903
Honus Wagner (.349)	1904
Honus Wagner (.339)	1906
Honus Wagner (.350)	1907
Honus Wagner (.354)	1908
Honus Wagner (.339)	1909
Honus Wagner (.334)	1911
Paul Waner (.380)	1927
Paul Waner (.362)	1934
Arky Vaughan (.385)	1935
Paul Waner (.373)	1936
Debs Garms (.355)	1940
Dick Groat (.325)	1960
Roberto Clemente (.351)	1961
Roberto Clemente (.339)	1964
Roberto Clemente (.329)	1965
Matty Alou (.342)	1966
Roberto Clemente (.357)	1967
Dave Parker (.338)	1977
Dave Parker (.334)	1978
Bill Madlock (.341)	1981
Bill Madlock (.323)	1983
Freddy Sanchez (.344)	2006

SOURCE: PITTSBURGH PIRATES

September 30, 2006: Freddy Sanchez batted .344 to win his first National League batting championship.

NOTABLE PIRATES

April 9, 2001: Fans gather around a statue of Pirates Hall of Famer Willie Stargell, as they wait to enter PNC Park for the Pirates' home opener against the Cincinnati Reds. Stargell, who led the Pirates to two World Series victories with his tape-measure homers, died earlier that day.

WARREN L. LEEDER/TRIBUNE-REVIEW

Willie Stargell

Outfielder/first baseman 1962-82

Stargell was a power hitter and beloved father figure to his teammates. During the 1979 championship season, he rewarded stellar efforts by giving players star patches. His teammates rewarded him with the nickname "Pops." Stargell's 475 home runs – hit over 21 years with the Pirates – remain the franchise's high-water mark. He knocked seven home runs over the right-field roof at Forbes Field and drove four homers into the right field upper deck of Three Rivers Stadium. In 1979, he won the National League, the National League Championship Series and the World Series Most Valuable Player awards. He is the only player to win all three in the same season. Born March 6, 1940, in Earlsboro, Oklahoma, he was inducted into the Hall of Fame in 1988. The Pirates honored him with a statue outside the brand-new PNC Park in 2001, though he didn't live to see the finished product.

Barry Bonds

Major League Baseball's home run king and Pirates outfielder 1986-92

Although controversy and steroid allegations have plagued Bonds, he still was one of baseball's best players during his 22-year career. In his years with the Pirates, Bonds won the first two of his seven National League Most Valuable Player awards and helped the team to three National League East division championships. Bonds left the Pirates after 1992 and signed a lucrative deal with his hometown San Francisco Giants. He was regarded as the best player of the 1990s. In the new century, he passed Hank Aaron in round-trippers to claim baseball's most cherished record, with 762 home runs. He was born July 24, 1964, in Riverside, California, and resides in San Francisco.

Roberto Clemente

outfielder 1955-72

Clemente was the first Latino player inducted into the Baseball Hall of Fame. He was an incredible fielder and hitter, as evidenced by his 12 Gold Gloves and 3,000 hits. Clemente, who was born August 18, 1934, in Puerto Rico, played his entire 18-year career in Pittsburgh with a lifetime batting average of .317. Clemente had a base hit in each of the 14 World Series games he played and was named the Most Valuable Player of the 1971 Series. In a city infatuated with sports, his achievements – and Clemente's highly praised sportsmanship – remain etched in the collective memory. Clemente died on December 31, 1972, in a plane crash delivering aid packages to victims of an earthquake in Nicaragua. The Hall of Fame waived its waiting period to posthumously elect Clemente into the Hall in 1973.

Ralph Kiner

outfielder 1946-53

In his 11-year major league career, Kiner spent eight with the Pirates and was one of the most feared hitters of his era. He led Major League Baseball in home runs for seven consecutive seasons from 1946 to 1952. Kiner topped 50 home runs twice, in 1947 and 1949. Kiner was traded to the Chicago Cubs after a salary dispute with General Manager Branch Rickey. He resides in San Diego, California. Born October 27, 1922, he was inducted into the Hall of Fame in 1975.

Bill Mazeroski

second baseman 1956-72

Mazeroski's career has been defined by a single event. In the bottom of the ninth inning of Game 7 of the 1960 World Series, the career .260 hitter knocked a Ralph Terry pitch over the wall at Forbes Field to break a 9-9 tie and defeat the vaunted New York Yankees for the championship. His heroics have never been copied in the seventh game of a World Series. Mazeroski's defensive prowess was the reason his career lasted as long as it did. He had a lifetime .983 fielding percentage and holds the record for career double plays turned by a second baseman at 1,706. He was inducted into the Hall of Fame in 2001. He was born September 5, 1936, in Wheeling, West Virginia, and resides in Greensburg.

Danny Murtaugh

manager 1957-64, 1967, 1970-71, 1973-76

As one of the franchise's most successful managers, Murtaugh was at the helm for the Pirates' World Series wins in 1970 and 1971. Before becoming a manager, he had a 10-year career as a second baseman in the majors. Murtaugh was twice named Manager of the Year by The Sporting News. With a 1,115-950 record, he is one of only 36 managers to win more than 1,000 games. He was born October 8, 1917, in Chester and died there on December 2, 1976.

Harold "Pie" Traynor

third baseman 1920-37

Traynor played before Gold Glove awards were handed out. Had he played in the current era, there's little doubt he would have won more than a few, as he is widely considered one of the greatest fielding third basemen in the history of the game.

Born November 11, 1899 in Framingham, Massachusetts, his nickname came from his fondness for pie. Traynor had a lifetime .320 average. He had 2,416 hits and batted in 1,273 runs. In 7,559 at bats, Traynor struck out only 278 times. In 1948, Traynor was selected to the Hall of Fame. He also managed the Pirates from 1934 to 1939. He died March 16, 1972, in Pittsburgh.

Honus Wagner

shortstop 1900-17

He was stocky, barrel-chested and bow-legged – and considered by some to be baseball's greatest player. Born February 24, 1874, in Chartiers, he led the Pirates to their first World Series title in 1909, led the National League in batting eight times and was one of the first five players inducted into the Hall of Fame. He was the second player to reach 3,000 hits, finishing his career with 3,415. Wagner died December 6, 1955, in Carnegie. His greatest legacy may be that of the T206 baseball card that bears his likeness wearing a uniform with the h-less "Pittsburg." Only a few cards were printed in the early 1900s, before Wagner refused the production of them. The scarcity of the card has made it the most valuable card in the world. In 2007, one sold for a record $2.8 million.

STEELERS

The Steelers are one of only three National Football League teams to win five Super Bowls, and they have become a model franchise.

But the Steelers weren't always synonymous with success and stability. From 1933 to 1970, the Steelers had just seven winning seasons.

The team is the fifth-oldest franchise in the NFL. Art Rooney Sr. purchased it on July 8, 1933, when the team was known as the Pirates. The name was changed to the Steelers in 1940.

To survive during the lean years of World War II, the team combined in 1943 with the Philadelphia Eagles and in 1944 with the Chicago Cardinals.

Fortunes changed when a young assistant by the name of Chuck Noll was hired as head coach in 1969 and was supplied with plenty of talent. The Steelers had one banner draft after another, and their haul in 1974 is arguably the best ever. It netted four future Pro Football Hall of Famers and provided the foundation for a run in which the Steelers won four Super Bowls in six seasons – 1974 and 1975; 1978 and 1979. The Steelers may well have added a fifth Super Bowl Championship had injuries not derailed them late in the '76 season.

As steel mills closed during the 1970s and Western Pennyslvania saw the out-migration of workers, the Steeler fan base spread, and "Steeler Nation" was born.

The Steelers finally got that elusive "one for the thumb" in the 2005 season when they made the playoffs as a No. 6 seed and made a stirring run that culminated with a 21-10 win over Seattle in Super Bowl XL.

A season after leading the Steelers to that championship, Crafton native Bill Cowher resigned as head coach. The Steelers hired 34-year-old Mike Tomlin to replace him, and Tomlin directed the team to an American Football Conference North title in his first season. He is just the third head coach the Steelers have had since 1969.

CHAZ PALLA/TRIBUNE-REVIEW

February 5, 2006: Super Bowl XL most valuable player Hines Ward displays the Lombardi Trophy awarded to the NFL champs.

Mel Blount's 57 career interceptions remain a Steelers record.

"Iron Mike" Webster anchored the Steelers offensive line for 150 straight games.

WILLIAM T. LARKIN

WILLIAM T. LARKIN

STEELERS IN THE HALL OF FAME

Nineteen Steelers have been inducted into the Pro Football Hall of Fame, including team founder Art Rooney Sr. and current team Chairman Dan Rooney.

Name	Position	Year Inducted	Length of career	Years in Pittsburgh
Burt Bell	co-owner	1963	1933-59	1940-45
Mel Blount	cornerback	1989	1970-83	1970-83
Terry Bradshaw	quarterback	1989	1970-83	1970-83
"Bullet" Bill Dudley	running back and defensive back	1966	1942-53	1942, 1945-46
Joe Greene	defensive tackle	1987	1969-81	1969-81; 2004-present (special assistant)
Jack Ham	linebacker	1988	1971-82	1971-82
Franco Harris	running back	1990	1972-84	1972-83
John Henry Johnson	fullback	1987	1954-66	1960-65
Walt Kiesling	player and coach	1966	1926-44, 1954-56	1937-39 (player); 1939-44, 1954-56 (coach)
Jack Lambert	linebacker	1990	1974-84	1974-84
Bobby Layne	quarterback	1967	1948-62	1958-62
Johnny "Blood" McNally	player and coach	1963	1925-39	1934 (player); 1937-39 (player and coach)
Chuck Noll	coach	1993	1960-91	1969-91
Art Rooney Sr.	owner and founder	1964	1933-88	1933-88
Dan Rooney	owner and chairman	2000	1955-present	1955-present
John Stallworth	wide receiver	2002	1974-87	1974-87
Ernie Stautner	defensive tackle	1969	1950-63	1950-63
Lynn Swann	wide receiver	2001	1974-82	1974-82
Mike Webster	center	1997	1974-90	1974-88

SOURCE: PITTSBURGH STEELERS

RETIRED JERSEYS

NAME	NUMBER
Ernie Stautner	70

KEITH HODAN/TRIBUNE-REVIEW

The statue of The Chief, Art Rooney Sr., sits outside Heinz Field.

February 7, 2006: Steelers fans pass safety Troy Polamalu over their heads during the city's celebration of the team's Super Bowl XL Championship.

January 1980: Lynn Swann celebrates his touchdown against the Los Angeles Rams in Super Bowl XIV, which the Steelers won 31-19.

NOTABLE STEELERS

Jerome Bettis
running back, 1996-2005

Owner of the most well-known and apt nicknames in the National Football League, "The Bus" was just that in his years with the Steelers. Bettis was a powerful runner between the tackles with surprisingly quick feet for a man his size. Spending 10 of his 13 NFL seasons with the Steelers, Bettis became the team's second-leading all-time rusher with 10,571 yards. At the start of the 2008 season, Bettis was the fifth-leading rusher in league history, with a career total of 13,662 yards. After debating retirement before the start of the 2005 season, Bettis decided to return to the field to make a run at Super Bowl XL, which would be held in Detroit, where he was born February 16, 1972. The team responded by embarking on a playoff run as a wild-card team and won the championship. Bettis announced his retirement immediately following the game. He resides in Roswell, Georgia, and maintains a home in Pittsburgh.

Terry Bradshaw
quarterback, 1970-83

As the leader of the 1970s Steelers' offense, Bradshaw has been one of the dynasty's most recognizable players. Bradshaw threw for 27,989 yards and 212 touchdowns in his 14-year career. His best work may have come in the postseason. In going 14-5 in the playoffs, he passed for 3,833 yards. He was named Most Valuable Player of Super Bowl XIII and Super Bowl XIV. He is one of only two quarterbacks to win four Super Bowls. He was inducted into the Pro Football Hall of Fame in 1989. Born September 2, 1948, in Shreveport, Louisiana, he resides in Texas.

Bill Cowher
head coach, 1992-2006

Born in Crafton, Cowher was hired by the Steelers to fill the void left by four-time Super Bowl winning coach Chuck Noll. It wasn't long until "Cowher Power" became the face of the franchise, as he led the team to the playoffs in his first six seasons. Cowher was 161-99-1 in his 15 seasons as coach. His teams won eight division championships and made 10 playoff appearances. Despite his years of success, Cowher was labeled as a coach who couldn't win the big one. The Steelers were 2-4 in AFC Championship games under Cowher and lost Super Bowl XXX. Cowher redeemed himself in 2006, when he finally brought a fifth league championship to Pittsburgh. Born May 8, 1957, in Pittsburgh, he resides in Raleigh, North Carolina.

"Bullet Bill" Dudley
running back, defensive back, 1942, 1945-46

The team's first round draft pick in 1942, he finished his rookie season as the NFL's leading rusher. He returned from World War II and in 1946 led the league in rushing, punt returns, interceptions and lateral pass attempts. That year he was named the NFL's Most Valuable Player. Born December 24, 1921, in Bluefield, Virginia, he was elected to the Hall of Fame in 1966.

Joe Greene
defensive tackle, 1969-81

The anchor of the famed "Steel Curtain" defense, Greene was the team's first draft pick in 1969 and was named the NFL's Rookie of the Year. He was elected to the Pro Bowl 10 times and earned all-NFL honors five times. He was twice the league's Defensive Player of the Year. In Super Bowl IX he intercepted a pass and recovered a fumble to help the team to its first Super Bowl Championship. He was born September 24, 1946, in Temple, Texas.

Jack Lambert
linebacker, 1974-84

Intelligence, speed, intensity – the undersized linebacker from Kent State University had all of these and became one of the most feared players in the game. His toothless grimace personified the Steeler defense. Lambert made the Pro Bowl nine times out of his 11 years in the NFL. He was named the league's Defensive Player of the Year in 1976. He was born July 8, 1952, in Mantua, Ohio and resides in Worthington in Armstrong County.

Chuck Noll
head coach, 1969-91

The architect of the 1970s Steelers dynasty ironically was born and raised in Cleveland, home of the arch-rival Browns. Noll's name is as closely associated with the Steelers as anyone owning the last name Rooney. Under Noll's reign, the team went from being a lovable loser to a perennial power, winning four Super Bowls in six seasons.

After retiring in 1991 with a record of 209-156-1, Noll was inducted into the Hall of Fame in 1993. Born on January 5, 1932, he resides in Hilton Head, South Carolina.

Ernie Stautner
defensive tackle, 1950-63

Stautner was considered one of the toughest players in the league. He won the NFL's best lineman award in 1957. He was named all-league four times and missed only six games in his 14 seasons with the team. He is the only Steeler to have his jersey retired. He was born April 20, 1925, in Germany and died on February 16, 2006.

Byron White
half back, 1938

Born June 18, 1916, in Fort Collins, Colorado, White gained fame playing at the University of Colorado. He was signed in 1938 by the Steelers – then known as the Pirates. He took 1939 off to study at Oxford as a Rhodes Scholar. He returned to play two seasons for the Detroit Lions in 1940 and 1941, his last seasons in the NFL. He led the league in rushing in 1938 and 1940. He joined the United States Navy during World War II. After the war, White entered Yale Law School. President John F. Kennedy nominated him to the United States Supreme Court, where he served as an associate justice from 1962 to 1993. He died April 15, 2002, in Denver.

December 23, 1972: Franco Harris eludes a tackle by Jimmy Ware of the Oakland Raiders to score the winning touchdown in the American Conference playoff game at Three Rivers Stadium. Harris' "Immaculate Reception" came when a desperation pass to a teammate bounced off a Raiders defender.

Franco Harris
running back, 1972-83

Harris could have done nothing after his rookie season in 1972 and still been a legend in Pittsburgh. He scored a touchdown in one of the most spectacular plays in NFL history, "The Immaculate Reception," to defeat the Oakland Raiders for the first playoff win in Steelers history. It was the start of a Hall of Fame career for Harris, who is the Steelers' all-time leading rusher with 11,950 yards. After winning the 1972 NFL Offensive Rookie of the Year award, he was elected to his first of nine consecutive Pro Bowl trips. The Penn State graduate was also the Most Valuable Player of Super Bowl IX. Born March 7, 1950, in Fort Dix, New Jersey, he resides in Leet Township.

PENGUINS

The Pittsburgh Penguins didn't have a founder. It had 21 of them, and those people invested $2 million to start the franchise in 1967.

In a sign of things to come, a request was made to hold that $2 million check a few extra days – just to collect the precious interest.

Money always has been an issue for the Penguins. Five months into their first season, the team was sold. Twice since then, they have been forced into bankruptcy.

But they have survived.

And thrived.

The Penguins twice have reached hockey's summit, winning Stanley Cups in 1991 and 1992 and falling just two games short of a championship in 2008.

Perhaps most remarkable is the parade of all-time greats – the march of the Penguins – through Pittsburgh over the years. Ten men with intimate connections to the franchise have been inducted into the Hockey Hall of Fame since 1991, most recently former star center Ron Francis in 2007. That doesn't include a sure-fire Hall of Famer in Jaromir Jagr and a couple of prodigious young talents, Sidney Crosby and Evgeni Malkin, who've extended the city's miraculous run of hockey prosperity.

The most amazing player of all was Mario Lemieux, now part-owner of the franchise. Lemieux twice rescued the team from near-certain departure, once in 1984, when he was drafted – and once in 1999, when he formed a group to buy the club out of bankruptcy.

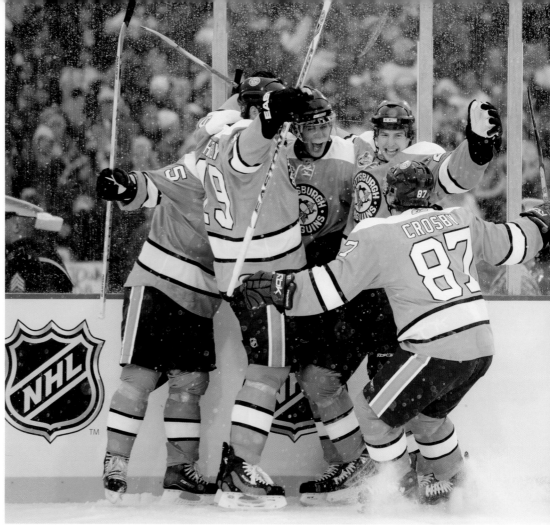

CHAZ PALLA/TRIBUNE-REVIEW

January 1, 2008: The Penguins celebrate Colby Armstrong's first-period goal against the Buffalo Sabres during the Winter Classic at Ralph Wilson Stadium in Orchard Park, New York.

PENGUINS IN THE HALL OF FAME

The first player with ties to the Penguins inducted into the National Hockey League Hall of Fame was Andy Bathgate. The former New York Ranger was chosen in the 1967 expansion draft.

Name	Position	Year Inducted	Length of career	Years in Pittsburgh
Andy Bathgate	right wing	1978	1952-75	1967-68, 1970-71
Leo Boivin	defenseman	1986	1952-70	1967-68
Scotty Bowman	coach	1991	1967-2002	1991-93
Herb Brooks	coach	2006	1981-2000	1999-2000
Paul Coffey	defenseman	2004	1980-2000	1987-92
Ron Francis	center	2007	1981-2004	1990-98
Tim Horton	defenseman	1977	1951-74	1971-72
Bob Johnson	coach	1992	1982-91	1990-91
Red Kelly	player and coach	1969	1947-67 (player), 1967-77 (coach)	1970-73
Mario Lemieux	center and owner	1997	1984-97, 2000-06 (player)	1984-present (player and owner)
Joe Mullen	right wing	2000	1979-97	1990-95, 1996-97
Larry Murphy	defenseman	2004	1980-2001	1990-95
Craig Patrick	general manager	2001	1980-2006	1989-2006
Glen Sather	left wing	1997	1966-77	1969-71
Bryan Trottier	center	1997	1975-94	1991-92, 1993-94

SOURCE: PITTSBURGH PENGUINS

2008: The Penguins sold out every home regular season game and all 11 playoff games for the first time in their history. Fans channeled their excitement into "white out" games during the playoffs.

October 1, 1997: Jaromir Jagr won the Art Ross Trophy as the NHL's leading point scorer five times while with the Penguins.

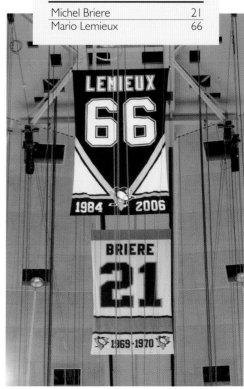

RETIRED JERSEYS

NAME	NUMBER
Michel Briere	21
Mario Lemieux	66

June 4, 2008: Evgeni Malkin kneels dejectedly after the Penguins lost to the Detroit Red Wings, 3-2, in Game 6 of the Stanley Cup Final.

February 23, 1975: Winger Rick Kehoe not only played for the Penguins but has been a scout, assistant coach and head coach.

December 8, 2000: Pittsburgh Penguins General Manager Craig Patrick was the architect of the team's two Stanley Cup Championships in the '90s.

ART ROSS TROPHY

Three Penguins have won
the Art Ross Trophy – the National
Hockey League scoring title:

NAME	SEASON
Mario Lemieux	1987-88
Mario Lemieux	1988-89
Mario Lemieux	1991-92
Mario Lemieux	1992-93
Jaromir Jagr	1994-95
Mario Lemieux	1995-96
Mario Lemieux	1996-97
Jaromir Jagr	1997-98
Jaromir Jagr	1998-99
Jaromir Jagr	1999-00
Jaromir Jagr	2000-01
Sidney Crosby	2006-07

SOURCE: PITTSBURGH PENGUINS

CHAZ PALLA/TRIBUNE-REVIEW

March 27, 2008: Sidney Crosby became the third Penguin to win an NHL scoring title.

December 31, 1988: Center Mario Lemieux celebrates scoring five goals, five different ways against the New Jersey Devils. Lemieux became the first and only player to score a goal at even strength, shorthanded, on the powerplay, on a penalty shot and into an empty net.

JAMES M. KUBUS/TRIBUNE-REVIEW

Mario Lemieux

center 1984-97, 2000-06; owner 1999-present

Lemieux was the best hockey player to play in Pittsburgh and one of the very best to play the game. He retired in 2006, ending his career with 690 goals and 1,033 assists, making him the seventh-highest scorer in National Hockey League history, despite the many injuries he suffered throughout his career. He was diagnosed with Hodgkin's lymphoma in 1993, from which he made a full recovery. In 1999, Lemieux bought the bankrupt franchise and moved it into the black. In 2007, he negotiated a deal to build a new arena for the team. He has also raised millions of dollars for his charity, the Mario Lemieux Foundation. He resides in Sewickley.

Michel Briere
center, 1969-70

He played only one season with the Penguins before his life was cut short. Drawing attention as a future star in the NHL, Briere scored 44 points as a 20-year-old Penguin rookie. In May 1970, Briere was in a car crash near his hometown of Marlartic, Quebec, that threw him from the back seat of the vehicle and caused major brain damage. He was in a coma for seven weeks and remained in a state that brought him in and out of consciousness for nearly a year. On April 13, 1971, he died at the age of 21. The Penguins have since retired Briere's number 21. The Quebec Major Junior Hockey League has since renamed its Most Valuable Player trophy after Briere.

Paul Coffey
defenseman, 1987-92

Coffey was another integral part of the Penguins' 1991 Stanley Cup Championship. After being traded to Pittsburgh in 1987, his superb offensive scoring power – uncommon among most defensemen – helped give the Penguins another weapon. He finished his career with 1,531 points. In 1986 while with the Edmonton Oilers, he scored 48 goals to set the single-season goal-scoring record for defensemen. He resides in Toronto.

Sidney Crosby
center, 2005-present

Crosby became the youngest player and only teenager to win a scoring title in any major North American sports league when he won the NHL scoring title in the 2006-07 season at 19. Chosen with the first pick in the 2005 NHL entry draft, he holds the franchise record for assists and points as a rookie. He is the youngest player in NHL history to score 100 points in a season. On May 31, 2007, he was named the Penguins' captain, making him the youngest captain in NHL history.

Ron Francis
center, 1990-98

Francis spent the majority of his career with the Hartford/Carolina franchise, but some of his best years came in Pittsburgh. After he was traded to the team in 1991, he helped the Penguins to their two Stanley Cup wins. Francis was an assist machine, recording 1,249 over his 24 seasons – the second best mark in NHL history. The center was perhaps just as known for his temperament. Throughout his career, Francis was regarded as one of the league's nicest players. His efforts helped earn him the Lady Byng Trophy three times. The award is annually given to the league's most gentlemanly player. He resides in North Carolina.

"Badger" Bob Johnson
coach, 1990-91

Johnson's brief time with the Penguins left an enormous impact on the organization. His bubbly personality made him charismatic and likable, and Johnson's knowledge of the game made him a successful coach at all levels of hockey, from high school to college and to the international level. It was with the Penguins that his career reached its zenith. He led the team to its first Stanley Cup win in 1991. He popularized the phrase "It's a great day for hockey." Tragedy would strike quickly, as Johnson died on November 26, 1991, from cancer. Johnson was inducted into the Hockey Hall of Fame in 1992. The Penguins dedicated the year to their deceased coach and won a second Stanley Cup.

Joe Mullen
right winger, 1990-95, 1996-97

Mullen stood 5-foot-9, but he was ferocious on the ice and played through injuries. His strong will helped him to become the first American to score 500 goals and record 1,000 points. His play seemed to pick up when he joined the Penguins in 1990. He had 17 postseason points in 1991, as the Penguins won their first Stanley Cup. In the following season, he recorded 42 goals. He retired in 1997 as the highest American scorer in the history of the NHL. He was inducted in the Hall of Fame in 2000 and resides in Pittsburgh.

1992: Penguins defenseman Larry Murphy photographs teammates flashing "two" to symbolize the team's second Stanley Cup Championship.

JAMES M. KUBUS/TRIBUNE-REVIEW

STADIUMS & ARENAS

LIBRARY OF CONGRESS

Exposition Park

Located on the North Shore near where Three Rivers Stadium would stand, Exposition Park was the Pirates' first home. It opened in 1882 and hosted the very first World Series in 1903 when the Pirates played the Boston Red Sox. The Pirates continued to play there until moving into Forbes Field midway through the 1909 season.

The Casino

The Casino, located at the entrance to Schenley Park, had the first artificial ice surface in North America. It opened in 1895, but burned to the ground in 1896.

CARNEGIE LIBRARY OF PITTSBURGH

1896: The Casino

Duquesne Gardens

In 1895 Pittsburgh political boss Christopher Lyman Magee purchased a 5-year-old street car barn at Fifth Avenue and Craig Street in Oakland and converted it into a multi-use arena capable of holding 5,000 people. The Duquesne Gardens became the premier ice hockey venue in Pittsburgh. The Gardens featured boxing matches, the Ice Capades – created by Pittsburgher John H. Harris – and, of course, hockey. It was the home of the short-lived National Hockey League Pittsburgh Pirates, but in its heyday it was the home of the minor league Pittsburgh Hornets. The Gardens came down in 1956 to make way for apartments and a restaurant.

CARNEGIE LIBRARY OF PITTSBURGH

Duquesne Gardens

Recreation Field

The first professional football game recognized by the National Football League was played at Recreation Field. On November 12, 1892, the Allegheny Athletic Association defeated the Pittsburgh Athletic Club 4-0 under the old points system. The Alleghenies paid William "Pudge" Heffelfinger, an all-American from Yale, $500 to play the game – infuriating Pittsburgh, which at first refused to play. The park was located on the North Side, northwest of present-day Heinz Field.

Forbes Field

Forbes Field was erected in Oakland in 1909 as the second steel-and-concrete structure in baseball. Originally built for the Pirates, it also hosted the Steelers and Pitt football. The Homestead Grays of the Negro Leagues also called Forbes Field home. Babe Ruth hit his last home run there. The stadium was vacated in 1970 when the Pirates returned to the North Side at Three Rivers Stadium. Home plate still sits, encased in glass. Part of the left-field wall, over which Bill Mazeroski's game-winning home run in the 1960 World Series sailed, has been preserved.

LIBRARY OF CONGRESS

1910: Forbes Field

Pitt Stadium

The University of Pittsburgh's on-campus stadium opened in 1925 for football and track-and-field events. It was home to the Pitt football team until 1999 when the Oakland stadium was razed to pave way for the Petersen Events Center. The Steelers played home games in Pitt Stadium from 1964 to 1969 until moving into Three Rivers Stadium.

STEVEN ADAMS/TRIBUNE-REVIEW

November 13, 1999: The final game at Pitt Stadium.

Three Rivers Stadium

Pittsburgh joined the trend of erecting multi-purpose sports facilities in 1970 when Three Rivers Stadium opened its doors on the North Side for the Pirates and Steelers. The Pittsburgh Maulers of the United States Football League played there for one season before folding. In its first decade, the stadium played host to two World Series and was home to Steelers teams that won four Super Bowls. The stadium became outdated with its lack of luxury suites and was demolished in 2001.

JAMES M. KUBUS/TRIBUNE-REVIEW

December 16, 2000: Fans packed Three Rivers Stadium to watch the Steelers take on the Washington Redskins for their final game in the 30-year-old stadium.

PNC Park

With the Pirates struggling financially and threatening to relocate, PNC Park, with its breathtaking views of the Allegheny River and the Downtown skyline, was opened in 2001 on the North Side as a means to keep the franchise healthy and stationed here. The park is often listed as one of the top three professional baseball venues in the country.

SIDNEY DAVIS/TRIBUNE-REVIEW

July 9, 2006: PNC Park

STEVEN ADAMS/TRIBUNE-REVIEW

February 11, 2001:
Implosion of Three Rivers Stadium

The old and the new

Ground was broken on August 14, 2008, for Pittsburgh's new sports arena. It will be the home of the Penguins and seat 18,087 for hockey – an increase of 1,147 seats. For basketball, it will hold 19,000.

The arena opened in 1961 in the Hill District as the Civic Arena. In December 1999 it became Mellon Arena. It was been home to the Penguins for 42 years.

The new arena will be across the street from Mellon Arena on the site of the old Saint Francis Medical Center.

STEVEN ADAMS/TRIBUNE-REVIEW

August 11, 2005: Heinz Field

Heinz Field

When it opened in 2001 nearly on the same spot as Three Rivers Stadium, Heinz Field became home for the Steelers and Pitt Panthers football teams. In terms of luxury boxes and club seating, Heinz Field is a vast upgrade over Three Rivers Stadium and Pitt Stadium. The Steelers have remained competitive in the new venue, regularly making the playoffs and winning the Super Bowl after the 2005 season.

JAMES M. KUBUS/TRIBUNE-REVIEW

August 14, 2008: Groundbreaking ceremony for Pittsburgh's new sports arena.

OTHER PITTSBURGH ATHLETES

Mike Ditka
Hall of Fame tight end

Born in Carnegie on October 18, 1939, Ditka was an All-American while playing for the University of Pittsburgh. He was the top draft pick of the Chicago Bears in 1961. He was an excellent blocker, but also caught 427 passes in his 12-year career. He was Rookie of the Year in 1961 and named to five straight Pro Bowls. He was a member of the Bears 1963 National Football League Championship team. He retired in 1972 after catching 43 career touchdown passes. He coached the Bears to a championship in Super Bowl XX. He was inducted into the Hall of Fame in 1988.

Tony Dorsett
Hall of Fame running back; Heisman Trophy winner at the University of Pittsburgh, 1973-76

Dorsett had a Hall of Fame career in the NFL. As a four-time All-American, his college career at Pitt was equally legendary. He became the school's only Heisman Trophy winner in 1976 – the same year the Panthers won the national championship – and he led the nation with 2,150 yards rushing. When he left Pitt, Dorsett's 6,526 career yards were the highest mark for any running back in history. Born April 7, 1954, Dorsett played at Hopewell Area High School in Beaver County. The school has since renamed its stadium in his honor. He was elected to the college and pro football halls of fame in the same year, 1994. He resides in Dallas.

Marshall Goldberg
University of Pittsburgh running back, 1935-39

Under legendary Pitt coach Jock Sutherland, Goldberg became one of the nation's top college running backs. Born on October 24, 1917, in Elkins, West Virginia, Goldberg came close to being the program's first Heisman winner, finishing third in the voting in 1937 and runner-up in 1938. He was an All-American in both of those seasons. Goldberg helped propel Pitt to national titles in 1936 and 1937. His 1,957 career rushing yards was the school record until Tony Dorsett broke it in 1974. He was elected to the College Football Hall of Fame in 1958. Goldberg also found success in the NFL as a member of the Chicago Cardinals. He died in Chicago on April 3, 2006.

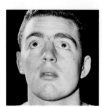

Don Hennon
University of Pittsburgh basketball player, 1955-59

At Wampum High School in Lawrence County, Hennon scored 2,376 points. When he got to Pitt, he continued to pour in points. Hennon made school basketball history in 1957, when he scored a 45 points against Duke – a record high against any opponent that still stands. Hennon's 24.2 career scoring average is still the highest in Pitt history. He is also the fourth-highest scorer in team history, with 1,841 points. All of his accomplishments were made before the 3-point line was instituted. Hennon, who stood 5 feet 6 inches, passed up a chance to play basketball professionally and became a surgeon. He resides in Franklin Park.

Johnny Majors
University of Pittsburgh football coach, 1973-76, 1993-96

Although he had a longer tenure as a coach at Tennessee, Majors' first four-year stint at Pitt was one of the most exciting times in the program's long history. Majors recruited some of the best talent ever on the school's roster, including Heisman-winning running back Tony Dorsett and quarterback Matt Cavanaugh. The talent translated into enormous success, as the team won the national championship in 1976 and Majors won coach of the year honors. He left to coach Tennessee, his alma mater in 1977. He returned to Pitt in 1993 but in four years was never able to match his previous success. He was born May 21, 1935, in Lynchburg, Tennessee and resides in Knoxville.

John "Red" Manning
Duquesne University men's basketball coach, 1958-74

Manning was a fixture at Duquesne. Along with serving as a coach for 16 seasons, he was a player and athletic director over his 33-year association with the school. Manning had just two losing seasons with the Dukes and had a 247-138 record. His teams made six trips to the postseason – twice to the National Collegiate Athletic Association Tournament and four times to the National Invitation Tournament. He left coaching after the 1973-74 season and was the school's athletic director until 1982. He was born on November 17, 1928, in Munhall and died April 27, 2005, in Bethel Park.

Dan Marino
Hall of Fame quarterback

With a quick release and a strong arm, Marino became the greatest quarterback in the histories of Central Catholic High School and the University of Pittsburgh, not to mention the NFL. Born September 15, 1961, in Oakland, he played at Central Catholic from 1976-79. Marino started in his freshman season at Pitt in 1979. Perhaps his shining moment there came in the 1982 Sugar Bowl. Marino tossed a 33-yard touchdown pass to tight end John Brown to defeat the University of Georgia, the defending national champions. In his 17-year career with the Miami Dolphins, Marino was selected to the Pro Bowl nine times. He still holds the record for most passing yards in a season, with 5,084. Marino was inducted into the Hall of Fame in 2005. He resides in Fort Lauderdale.

Joe Montana
Hall of Fame quarterback

After his senior year at Ringgold High School in Washington County, Montana accepted a scholarship to play at Notre Dame. Drafted in the third round by the San Francisco 49ers, he began one of the greatest careers in NFL history. He was named league Most Valuable Player twice, elected to the Pro Bowl eight times and selected to the Hall of Fame in 2000. His four Super Bowl wins matched Terry Bradshaw, the only other quarterback to achieve the feat. Montana never threw an interception in a Super Bowl and won three Most Valuable Player awards, both unrivaled accomplishments. Born June 11, 1956, a native of Monongahela, he resides in Clayton, California.

Stan Musial

Hall of Fame left fielder

In the St. Louis Cardinals' storied history, Musial's name is the most revered. The son of immigrant steelworkers in Donora, Musial played high school baseball with Ken Griffey Jr.'s grandfather. From 1941 to 1963, Musial won three World Series with the Cardinals and claimed as many National League Most Valuable Player awards. His 3,680 hits are the fourth-best total all-time, and he had a lifetime batting average of .331. He was elected to the Hall of Fame in his first year of eligibility in 1969. He was born November 21, 1920, in Donora and resides in St. Louis.

Joe Namath

Hall of Fame quarterback

Namath's biggest claim to fame will always be his guarantee of victory before Super Bowl III against the heavily favored Baltimore Colts. The New York Jets quarterback completed 17 of 28 passes for 208 yards and was named the Most Valuable Player. For his career, Namath threw for 27,663 yards and 173 touchdowns. He was a five-time Pro Bowl selection. He was inducted into the Hall of Fame in 1985. Namath was born May 31, 1943, in Beaver Falls. He resides in Tequestsa, Florida.

Norm Nixon

Duquesne University men's basketball point guard, 1974-77

Nixon leads the Dukes in career field goals made with 753 and is tops in career assists with 577. His success at Duquesne led to the Los Angeles Lakers making him a first-round pick in the 1977 National Basketball Association draft. He won two league championships with the Lakers, made the All-Star team twice and finished with 12,065 points and 6,386 assists. He serves as a television analyst for Lakers games on Fox Sports Net West. He resides in Los Angeles.

Arnold Palmer

Western Pennsylvania's most famous golfer

A winner of seven major tournaments throughout the late 1950s and 1960s, Palmer is considered one of the greatest golfers of all time. He has been largely credited with helping spread the popularity of golf into the mainstream. Palmer was the Professional Golfers' Association of America's Player of the Year in 1960 and 1962 and was the leading money winner on the tour in 1958, 1960, 1962 and 1963. After his prime years, Palmer was instrumental in the development of the Senior PGA Tour. He founded a world-class medical facility, Arnold Palmer Hospital for Children in Orlando, Florida. Not forgetting his Western Pennsylvania roots, Palmer also founded the Arnold Palmer Pavilion, which is the University of Pittsburgh Medical Center Cancer Center in Latrobe. He was born September 10, 1929, in Latrobe.

Charles Smith

University of Pittsburgh men's basketball forward, 1984-88

Smith is Pitt's all-time leading scorer with 2,045 points. Among the Big East's top 50 players, Smith is listed eighth. In 1985, he was named the Big East Conference's Freshman of the Year. In 1988, he was the league's player of the year. He led Pitt to two regular-season conference championships. The power forward won a bronze medal at the 1988 Summer Olympics. That year, he also became the first Pitt player ever taken in the first round of the NBA draft. He resides in New Jersey.

Johnny Unitas

Hall of Fame quarterback

Unitas' football career was destined not to blossom in his hometown. He was born in Pittsburgh on May 7, 1933, and grew up on Mount Washington. He was drafted by the Steelers in 1955, but was released before the season began. In spite of some early setbacks, Unitas became one of the NFL's all-time greats with the Baltimore Colts. In an era when seasons were only 12 or 14 games, Unitas became the first signal-caller to reach 40,000 career yards passing. He also set one of the league's most resilient records, by throwing a touchdown pass in 47 consecutive games. A record that still stands. In 1958, Unitas won his only NFL Championship in overtime against the New York Giants, considered one of the greatest games in league history. He was inducted into the Hall of Fame in 1979. Unitas died on September 11, 2002, in Timonium, Maryland.

June 20, 1946: Referee Eddie Joseph calls a halt during the World Heavyweight Championship rematch as challenger Billy Conn goes down in the sixth round against Joe Louis at Yankee Stadium.

BOXING

Pittsburghers left their mark on professional boxing throughout the 1920s, '30s and '40s.

Billy Conn, the original "Pittsburgh Kid," won the light heavyweight championship in 1939. However it was his 1941 fight with heavyweight champion Joe Louis that brought him celebrity. Conn was ahead on points when Louis knocked him out in the thirteenth round.

Fritzie Zivic had a cross-town rivalry with Conn. Zivic won the welterweight crown when he upset Henry Armstrong in Madison Square Garden in 1940.

Harry Greb, "The Human Windmill," held the middleweight and light heavyweight championships in the 1920s. He fought about 300 fights and was the only man to have defeated Gene Tunney.

Sammy Angott of Washington won the world lightweight title in 1941. At the time five of the eight boxers with world championship titles were from Western Pennsylvania.

OLYMPIANS

Kurt Angle
Gold medal wrestler

Angle was an all-state linebacker at Mount Lebanon High School, but it was wrestling where he found his greatest triumphs. After winning a state championship as a senior in 1987, Angle went to Clarion University of Pennsylvania, where he won two National Collegiate Athletic Association titles. In 1996, Angle sustained a severe neck and back injury during the Olympic trials, though he would go on to win. After rehabilitating for five months, he still felt intense pain. Nevertheless, Angle won the gold medal for freestyle wrestling in the heavyweight division at the 1996 Summer Olympics in Atlanta. Angle resides in Moon.

Roger Kingdom
Gold medal hurdler

Kingdom attended the University of Pittsburgh on a football scholarship but excelled at track. In 1984, Kingdom won a gold medal in the 110-meter hurdles at the Los Angeles Games, a feat he matched in Seoul in 1988. He set a world-record time in the event in 1989, which stood until 1993 and was the United States record until 2006. Kingdom lives in Monroeville and serves as head coach for track and field at California University of Pennsylvania.

Herbert Douglas Jr.
Bronze medal long jumper

Douglas grew up idolizing Olympic gold medalist John Woodruff, who befriended the young track star in 1940. Douglas became the first person in Western Pennsylvania to win three high school state championships in track and field. In 1948, the first Olympic games after World War II, Douglas took the bronze medal. He earned bachelor's and master's degrees from the University of Pittsburgh and became vice president of Schieffelin & Company, a wine and spirits importer. He is an emeritus trustee at Pitt and resides in Philadelphia.

Swin Cash
Gold medalist, women's basketball

Cash was a standout basketball player at McKeesport High School and played in college for Connecticut's elite women's program. There, she helped the team win national titles in 2000 and 2002. In 2002 as a senior, Cash helped lead the Huskies to a 39-0 season – one of the greatest seasons in women's basketball history. She was drafted by the Women's National Basketball Association's Detroit Shock in 2002 and promptly helped the team to its first championship in 2003. Cash won a gold medal with the United States women's basketball team in the 2004 Summer Olympics in Athens. She resides in Seattle.

Lauryn Williams
Olympic silver medal sprinter

Lauryn Williams, a native of Rochester in Beaver County, won a silver medal in the 100-meter dash during the 2004 Olympics in Athens. In 2004, she ran the 100 meters in 10.97 seconds at the national championships, which was the second-fastest time in the world that year. She resides in Miami.

John Woodruff
Gold medal runner

Woodruff rose to national prominence with one of the most exciting races in Olympic history. In 1936, he was a freshman at the University of Pittsburgh and won a spot in the 800 meters on the United States Olympic team. The Olympics were held in Berlin, with Adolf Hitler predicting the games would showcase Aryan supremacy. Woodruff was the favorite in the 800 meters. In the finals, he was boxed in by competitors running at a slower pace. Woodruff stopped and let his competition run around him, then sped up and came from behind to win the gold medal. He also won three collegiate track titles. Woodruff was born July 5, 1915, in Connellsville and died October 30, 2007, in Fountain Hills, Arizona.

March 23, 2001: Oakland Catholic head coach Suzie McConnell-Serio celebrates the Eagles' PIAA Class AAAA victory over Council Rock Friday night in Hershey.

Suzie McConnell-Serio

Gold and bronze medalist, women's basketball

McConnell-Serio played at Seton-LaSalle High School from 1980 to 1984. In her senior season, she led Seton-La Salle to a state championship. She played at Penn State from 1984 to 1988 and became the school's inaugural first-team All-American. She was part of the gold medal-winning United States women's basketball team in the 1988 Olympics and a member of the team that took a bronze in 1992. McConnell-Serio also played three seasons in the WNBA. As a high school coach, McConnell-Serio led Oakland Catholic to state titles in 1993, 2001 and 2003. After the 2002-03 season, she left the school to coach in the WNBA. She returned to coaching in Pittsburgh in 2007 to head the Duquesne University women's program. In June 2008, McConnell-Serio was inducted into the Women's Basketball Hall of Fame.

2008: The interior of the Grand Concourse Restaurant in Station Square has been called a city treasure. Built in 1901 as waiting room for the Pennsylvania & Lake Erie Railroad Station, the two-story hall is embellished with ornate detail that conjures images of a bygone era.

CHAPTER 11

STEVEN ADAMS/TRIBUNE-REVIEW

uniquely Pittsburgh

Now you see it, now you don't – the *h* at the end of Pittsburgh.

When General John Forbes renamed the ruins of Fort Duquesne in 1758, he called the outpost Pittsbourgh, in honor of English Prime Minister William Pitt. Forbes was a Scot, and -burgh and -bourgh were used in Scotland as variations of borough.

Well, the *o* disappeared, but the *h* stuck.

In 1890, the United States Board on Geographic Names dropped the *h* from all cities and towns ending with -burgh. The decision was not popular here. In 1911, bowing to public pressure, the Board on Geographic Names restored the *h* to Pittsburgh.

June 24, 2005: A cool spot on a hot day – the wave pool at Settler's Cabin Park, which is the most popular of Allegheny County's three wave pools. The park, by the way, got its name from the 1780 Walker-Ewing log cabin nestled within the park's 1,610 acres.

August 8, 2007: Birds of a feather flock together at the National Aviary, built on the site of the original Western Penitentiary, which opened in 1827 and closed in 1880. The aviary, in the North Side, is home to more than 500 birds from around the world.

May 30, 2007: The Pittsburgh Zoo & PPG Aquarium opened June 14, 1898, as the Highland Park Zoological Gardens. The zoo is home to more than 400 species, including 22 that are threatened or endangered.

July 5, 2000: The Pirate Parrot struts his stuff in Market Square, Downtown. The parrot debuted in 1979 and is one of the most recognizable mascots in sports.

July 18, 2003.: A "sammich" from Primanti Brothers comes topped with fries, cole slaw and tomato. It's a Pittsburgh tradition since the Depression.

April 4, 2005: What's a Pirates game without racing pierogies n'at? Jalapeno Hanna, Oliver Onion and Chester Cheese.

January 19, 2005: The late Myron Cope, the beloved voice of the Steeler Nation, created the Terrible Towel. Cope once quipped that his nasal voice "falls upon the public's ears like china crashing from shelves in an earthquake."

JASMINE GOLDBAND/TRIBUNE-REVIEW

TRIBUNE-REVIEW

January 25, 2006: Beer here: Iron City Beer has been brewed in Pittsburgh since 1861 and in the brewery at Liberty Avenue and 34th Street since 1866. These cans honor the 1970s Steelers.

HEIDI MURRIN/TRIBUNE-REVIEW

September 7, 2003: The Majestic, the flagship of the Gateway Clipper Fleet, sails by a packed Heinz Field during the Steelers season opener against the Baltimore Ravens. Steelers won, 34-15.

July 16, 2002: Waters dance at The Fountain at Bessemer Court in Station Square in the South Side. Station Square was once the headquarters of the Pennsylvania & Lake Erie Railroad. After the railroad no longer needed the property, the Pittsburgh History & Landmarks Foundation developed it into office and retail space with initial funding from Richard M. Scaife's Allegheny Foundation.

February 2, 2004: Pittsburgh averages 153 days a year of measurable rainfall – about 38 inches of rain annually. The number of clear, sunny days averages 59 ...

February 13, 2006: ... And the number of days with an inch or more of snow averages just 12 each year.

June 1, 2007: Is he: celebrating a pay raise, thinking he needs to call a personal injury attorney or dancing in a performance of the Pittsburgh Dance Alloy at the Three Rivers Arts Festival?

May 5, 2007: Yes, the reason we love bingo is that it was invented here in 1924 by Hugh J. Ward of Hazelwood.

June 5, 2005: Roller coasters rule at Kennyw-o-o-o-o-d Park (and have since the first coaster opened there in 1902)!

July 2, 2006: No, they didn't take a wrong turn at Stanwix Street. It's the Pittsburgh Three Rivers Regatta's "Anything That Floats Race."

January 1, 2005: The hearty souls of the Pittsburgh Polar Bear Club welcome each New Year's Day with a dip in the Monongahela River. The water this day was a balmy 38 degrees.

April 18, 2006: Water from the Point State Park fountain can shoot to a height of 250 feet when all three pumps are running. Most days two pumps operate, and the water reaches a height of 100 to 150 feet. The fountain was dedicated August 30, 1974, marking completion of the 36-acre park, which took 29 years to design and construct.

Acknowledgements, references and sources:

Allegheny Conference on Community Development

Allegheny County's Hundred Years, by George H. Thurston; A.A. Anderson & Son, 1888

Allegheny Foundation

Leland D. Baldwin, Mississippi Valley Historical Review, June 1933

Baseball Almanac

Beyond the Shadow of the Senators: The Untold Story of the Homestead Grays and the Integration of Baseball, by Brad Snyder, The McGraw-Hill Companies, 2003

Regis Bobonis Sr., vice president of the Daniel B. Matthews Historical Society of Sewickley

Buildings of Pennsylvania: Pittsburgh and Western Pennsylvania, by Lu Donnelly, H. David Brumble IV and Franklin Toker, University of Virginia Press, forthcoming in 2009

Carnegie Library of Pittsburgh
With special thanks to:
The Pennsylvania Department

Carnegie Mellon University

Carnegie Museums of Pittsburgh

The Carthage Foundation

Case Study: Redevelopment of A Former Army Ammunition Plant Located in the Hays Community of Pittsburgh, Pennsylvania, by J.P. Barton, Department of Civil & Environmental Engineering, Carnegie Mellon University, June 17, 1996

Chatham University

Children's Museum of Pittsburgh

College Football Hall of Fame

Congressional Medal of Honor Society

Linda Deafenbaugh, program coordinator, Pennsylvania Ethnic Heritage Studies Center

Don't Call Me Boss, by Michael P. Weber, University of Pittsburgh Press, 1988

Drake Well Museum

Duquesne University

East Allegheny Community Council

Famous Men and Women of Pittsburgh, Pittsburgh History & Landmarks Foundation, 1981

The Frick Art & Historical Center

Hagley Museum and Library, Wilmington, Delaware

Healing Body, Mind, and Spirit: The History of the St. Francis Medical Center, Pittsburgh, Pennsylvania, by Carolyn Leonard Carson, Carnegie Mellon University Press, 1995

The Heinz Endowments

Senator John Heinz History Center
With special thanks to:
Samuel Black, curator of African American Collections
Rachel Colker, consulting curator

A History of Allegheny County, Pennsylvania, A. Werner & Co., 1889

History of Pittsburgh and Environs, by George Thornton Fleming, American Historical Society Incorporated, 1922

A History of Trade Unionism in the United States, by Selig Perlman, The McMillen Company, 1922

Hockey Hall of Fame

Inheritors of a Glorious Reality A History of Shadyside Hospital, by Mary Brignano, 1991

International Boxing Hall of Fame

Johnstown Area Heritage Association

The Life and Legacy of Rachel Carson, by Linda Lear, 1998

The Life and Speeches of Henry Clay, Volume 1, by Henry Clay, James Barrett Swain; Greeley & McElrath, 1843

Kelly Linn, curator, Fort Pitt Block House

Charles McCollester, founder of the Pennsylvania Center for the Study of Labor Relations, Indiana University of Pennsylvania

Manchester Historic Society

The Mattress Factory

Edward K. Muller, professor of history, University of Pittsburgh

National Aeronautics and Space Administration

National Baseball Hall of Fame

National Basketball Association

National Football League

National Italian American Sports Hall of Fame

National Weather Service

Negro League Baseball Players Association

New Pittsburgh Courier

Pennsylvania, Colonial and Federal: A History, 1603-1903, by Howard Malcolm Jenkins, Pennsylvania Historical Publishing Association, 1903

Pennsylvania Historical and Museum Commission

Pennsylvania State Archives

Pennsylvania Railroad Technical and Historical Society

Pennsylvania's Black History, by Charles L. Blockson, Philadelphia, Portfolio Associates, Inc., 1975

The City of Pittsburgh

Pittsburgh and Allegheny in the Centennial Year, by George H. Thurston, A.A. Anderson & Son, 1876

Pittsburgh Born, Pittsburgh Bred, researched, written and edited by C. Prentiss Orr, Abby Mendelson and Tripp Clarke, published in cooperation with the Senator John Heinz History Center, 2008

A Pittsburgh Composer and His Memorial, by Fletcher Hodges Jr., The Historical Society of Western Pennsylvania, 1951

Pittsburgh During the Civil War: 1860 to 1865, by Arthur B. Fox, Mechling Bookbindery, 2002

Pittsburgh History & Landmarks Foundation
With special thanks to:
Frank Stroker, assistant archivist
Arthur P. Ziegler Jr., president

Pittsburgh in Stages Two Hundred Years of Theater, by Lynne Conner, University of Pittsburgh Press, 2007

Pittsburgh Penguins

Pittsburgh Pirates

Pittsburgh Steelers

Pittsburgh, The Story of an American City, by Stefan Lorant, Authors Edition, Inc., 1980

Pittsburgh Tribune-Review

Pittsburgh's Landmark Architecture: The Historic Buildings of Pittsburgh and Allegheny County, by Walter C. Kidney, Pittsburgh History & Landmarks Foundation, 1997

PittsburghNeighborhoodsTours.com

Pro Football Hall of Fame

Railroad Museum of Pennsylvania

The Rivers of Steel National Heritage Area
With special thanks to:
Ronald Baraff, director of museum collections and archives
Tiffani Emig, curator of collections

F. Brooks Robinson Jr., vice president of marketing, Regional Industrial Development Corporation

Saint Vincent College

San Francisco Giants

Sarah Scaife Foundation

Second Geological Survey of the Monongahela River Region, by J. Sutton Wall, 1884.

Sisters of Saint Francis

Society for the Preservation of the Duquesne Heights Incline

The Standard History of Pittsburg, Pennsylvania, edited by Erasmus Wilson, H.R. Cornell Co., 1898

Joel A. Tarr, Richard S. Caliguiri University Professor of History and Policy, Carnegie Mellon University

The Testimony of William Hunter Dammond: The First African American Graduate of the University of Pittsburgh, by Roland Barksdale-Hall, The Journal of Pan African Studies, June 2007.

Through the Years with the Nurses at the Shadyside Hospital, by Miriam C. Miller, Davis & Warde, Inc., 1946

United States Army Corps of Engineers
With special thanks to:
Werner Loehlein, chief of the water management branch, Pittsburgh

United States Mine Rescue Association

The University of Pittsburgh
With special thanks to:
The Athletic Department

University of Pittsburgh Medical Center

USA Track & Field

J.R. Weldin Company

The Western Pennsylvania Conservancy

The Western Pennsylvania Hospital

Roger Westman

Women's National Basketball Association

World Affairs Council of Pittsburgh

Art:

Fly sheet: The transparency just inside the front cover enables you to compare the young Pittsburgh with the city today. The first image is William Coventry Wall's lithograph of Mrs. E. C. Gibson's *Pittsburgh in 1817*, based on a sketch she made here during her honeymoon. It is superimposed over Steven Adams' photograph of the Point taken in September, 2008.

Page 13: Selden I. Davis, American, 1904-1971 *Pittsburghesque*, 1946 gelatin silver print, 16 1/8 x 12 7/16 in. Carnegie Museum of Art, Pittsburgh; Second Century Acquisition Fund Photograph ©2008 Carnegie Museum of Art, Pittsburgh

Page 24: Luke Swank, American, 1890-1944, *[Filling Molds with Molten Iron II]* c.1934, vintage gelatin silver print, 13 1/4 x 10 3/8 in., Carnegie Museum of Art, Pittsburgh; Gift of Edith Swank Long by transfer from the Pennsylvania Department, Carnegie Library of Pittsburgh Photograph ©2008 Carnegie Museum of Art, Pittsburgh

Page 53: Everett Raymond Kinstler, *Portrait of Sarah Mellon Scaife*, 1974, American/ b.1926, Oil on canvas 38 1/8 x 34 1/8 in. Carnegie Museum of Art, Pittsburgh; Gift of James M. Bovard

Page 104: Aaron Henry Gorson (1872-1933), *Pittsburgh at Night*, 1926, American. Oil on canvas 34 x 36 in.

Page 105: John Kane (1860-1934), *Self-portrait*, 1929, American, born Scotland. Oil on canvas over composition board, 91.7 x 68.8 cm. Museum of Modern Art, New York, NY; Abby Aldrich Rockefeller Fund; licensed by SCALA/Art Resource, New York, NY